Praise for *Qui*

"A compelling mix of science, social critique, and pragmatism, *Quitting: A Life Strategy* upends the dominant narratives about giving up. Sometimes stepping back really is the right way to move forward in life."

– Cal Newport, *New York Times* bestselling author of *Digital Minimalism* and *A World Without Email*

"Julia Keller has flipped the script on one of the most aligned human acts: quitting. Before you decide to stick with it, gut it out, or see it through, consider the stories and evidence in *Quitting: A Life Strategy* and give yourself permission to walk away."

– Bruce Feiler, *New York Times* bestselling author of *Life is in the Transitions*

"The world needs more quitters. In her fabulous new book, Julia Keller lays out the compelling case for quitting – explaining why we should quit sooner and more often, and also how to quit. *Quitting: A Life Strategy* is as entertaining as it is important."

– Steven Levitt, *New York Times* bestselling author of *Freakonomics*

"Julia Keller's *Quitting: A Life Strategy* offers a timely corrective in a world that's forever telling us to do (and endure) more. This book is a celebration of people learning their limits, standing by their boundaries, and forging new paths when old, back breaking ways of being have failed them."

– Dr. Devon Price, author of *Laziness Does Not Exist*

"*Quitting: A Life Strategy* is a thoughtful book that challenges conventional wisdom about giving up, blending scientific research with stories of real life decisions to show how quitting can actually be a powerful way to take control of your life."

— Joseph T. Hallinan, Pulitzer Prize winning journalist and bestselling author of *Why We Make Mistakes*

"In her beguiling mix of uncanny insight, scientific evidence and human stories, Julia Keller debunks America's deeply ingrained faith in perseverance – in a book that's just unquittable."

— *Elizabeth Taylor, coauthor of American Pharoah: Richard J. Daley - His Battle for Chicago and the Nation*

"Julia Keller weaves science, pop culture, and scholarship into a forceful and often funny book that finally settles the argument: winners DO quit. Keller's book proves that whether you're an impetuous Jerry Maguire type or react with the speed of a slime mold, quitting will be the launchpad into the liberating realm of 'what's next.'"

— Amy Dickinson, nationally syndicated advice columnist ("Ask Amy") and *New York Times* bestselling author

QUITTING:
A Life Strategy

The Myth of Perseverance—and
How the New Science of
Giving Up Can Set You Free

Dr Julia Keller

First published in the United States in 2023 by Balance
An imprint of Grand Central Publishing
A division of Hachette Book Group, Inc

First published in Great Britain in 2023 by Yellow Kite
An imprint of Hodder & Stoughton
An Hachette UK company

1

Jacket design by Shreya Gupta. Jacket image by Getty Images.

A CIP catalogue record for this title is available from the British Library

Trade Paperback ISBN 9781399714730
eBook ISBN 9781399714723

Typeset in Adobe Garamond Pro by Manipal Technologies Limited

Printed and bound in Great Britain by Clays Ltd, Elcograf S.p.A.

Hodder & Stoughton policy is to use papers that are natural, renewable and recyclable
products and made from wood grown in sustainable for-ests. The logging and manufacturing
processes are expected to conform to the environmental regulations of the country of origin.

Yellow Kite
Hodder & Stoughton Ltd
Carmelite House
50 Victoria Embankment
London EC4Y 0DZ

www.yellowkitebooks.co.uk

To Annie Kate Goodwin
1986–2019

You see, you cannot draw lines and compartments, and refuse to budge beyond them. Sometimes you have to use your failures as stepping-stones to success. You have to maintain a fine balance between hope and despair...in the end, it's all a question of balance.

—*Rohinton Mistry,* A Fine Balance

No matter how far you have gone down the wrong path, turn back.

—*Proverb*

Contents

PART III
Giving Up: A How-to Guide

Introduction

By doing nothing, we change nothing. And
by changing nothing, we hang on to what we
understand, even if it is the bars of our own jail.

—John le Carré

Quitting is an act of love.

It's also an escape hatch, a long shot, a shortcut, a leap of imagination, a fist raised in resistance, a saving grace, and a potential disaster—because it may backfire in spectacular ways, sabotaging careers and blowing up relationships. It can ruin your life.

And it can save it, too.

All in all, though, it's a gesture of generosity toward yourself and your future, a roundabout way of saying, "Not this. Not now. But later...*something else.*"

You might not see quitting in such a positive light. I get it: For a long time, I didn't see it that way, either. In fact, that's not even *close* to how I viewed the prospect of giving up as I sat cross-legged on the grimy linoleum floor of a studio apartment in Morgantown, West Virginia, one memorable night, weeping with abandon, tormented by the need to make a drastic change but fearing the judgment that would ensue, wondering how I could possibly endure the next ten minutes—much less the rest of my life.

Later, I would play this low point for laughs. Years after the fact, I'd make a joke out of it: "Just imagine," I'd say, "me at nineteen, huddled on the floor, crying my eyes out and using a bath towel to blow my nose—because a Kleenex just wasn't up to the job. Drama queen alert!"

When I entertained friends with the story of my initial foray into graduate school, which had necessitated leaving home and living on my own for the very first time, I'd whip out fancy words like "disconsolate" and "bereft" and melodramatic phrases like "fathomless despair." I'd roll my eyes and snicker at the picture of silly old me.

But at the time it was happening, I didn't snicker. Because it wasn't amusing. Making fun of the memory was a way of walling off the raw misery of that moment: I really did sit on a dirty floor and sob into a giant towel, overwhelmed by a hopelessness so sweeping and intense that I could barely breathe. Classes had just gotten underway at West Virginia University, where I was employed as a graduate teaching assistant while pursuing a doctoral degree in English literature. Things were not, as you may have inferred by now, going well.

I was lonely and desperately homesick. I hated my classes—both the ones I was taking and the ones I was teaching. I hated the university. I hated my apartment. I hated Morgantown. In short, I hated everything—especially myself. Because I believed I ought to be able to handle this. In theory, grad school had seemed like a perfect fit, even though I was younger (and as soon became clear, appallingly less mature) than a typical grad student. But here in the real world, it was a different story. I couldn't stop the torrent of negative emotions. And giving up wasn't an option. Giving up would mean I was a loser.

A bum.

A washout.

That night—the night of the Tragically Soggy Towel—I'd plunged to an emotional rock bottom. I bounced once, twice, three times, then stuck there. I gave up and called home. My father answered.

"I can't do this," I said, blubbering and snuffling. "I just can't."

I fully expected him to reply, *Don't be such a baby. Stick it out. You'll be a better person for it.* But my dad, a mathematics professor who under normal circumstances was a hard taskmaster with no sympathy for snivelers, must've sensed that a tough-love pep talk—*Suck it up, Buttercup!*—wasn't what I needed right then.

In a gentle voice, he replied, "It's a three-hour drive. I'll be there in three hours."

I spent the next month or so hunkered down in my bedroom in the home I'd grown up in, afraid that if my friends found out I was back—that I'd bailed on my fellowship and flat-out fled—I'd be branded a quitter. And probably ostracized. I decided to beat them to the punch and ostracized myself.

Gradually, I began to feel a little better. I applied for writing internships. I ended up in Washington, DC, working for investigative journalist Jack Anderson. That, in turn, led to a job at a small-town newspaper, which led to a job at a bigger newspaper. Finally, I ended up at the *Chicago Tribune*, where my work won a Pulitzer Prize.

Yet as I sat there on that sticky floor with a towel clutched in one hand and a phone in the other, filled with dread as I contemplated calling home and admitting defeat, I wanted to tough it out. I summoned up the memory of every motivational speech I'd ever heard, every bright and shiny aphorism. I tried to be my own personal drill sergeant, giving myself firmly worded pep talks:

You can do it!
But I couldn't.
And so I quit.

———————

If I had to choose the catalyst for this book, I'd put my finger right there: the night in Morgantown when I sat in a defeated heap, shaking with sobs and wondering what was going to become of me.

Giving up was survival instinct, pure and simple. Yet before I was able to even consider doing it, I had to override a ton of powerful messages, the ones that tell us there's something weak and shameful and cowardly about quitting—even when we're emotionally and spiritually hollowed out. My mind and my body were offering me clear, unmistakable signals that I simply wasn't ready to be a grad student at that point. Later, yes: I earned a doctoral degree at the Ohio State University. But not there. And not then.

Better days eventually came along, but only after I'd screeched to a dead halt, healed a bit, and finally moved forward—well, maybe sideways—when the time was right. Only after I'd berated myself for being a shiftless lout. Only after I'd called myself all kinds of ugly names:

Screwup. Sissy. Dumbass. Chickenshit.

Only after I'd sat in my bedroom for a while, wincing when I looked in the mirror—because what I saw was a girl who lacked grit. Who didn't persevere. Who couldn't cut it.

Later, I began to wonder: Why had I put myself through such an ordeal? Not the ordeal of *going* to grad school, mind you, but the psychological hell that commenced when I decided to *quit* grad school. Why did I engage in such ferocious self-loathing? Weren't things bad enough already?

I understood *why* I'd felt that way—quitting reeks of capitulation, of surrender—but I couldn't figure out where such a strange notion had originated in the first place. Who says that quitting is ill-advised? When and where and why did the idea arise? The animals with whom we share the planet aren't burdened with an anti-quit bias. They keep their eyes on the prize: survival. If an activity isn't working, if it isn't providing sustenance, they quit without a backward glance. They *have* to—if they want to live. Expending too much energy in a futile pursuit leaves them spent and, hence, vulnerable to predators. And we human beings are at our best when we do the same—when we quickly reassess strategies that aren't getting us anywhere and we make changes on the fly as often as we need to.

Yet the cultural marching orders we receive firmly command the opposite: *Whatever you do*, we're told, *don't quit*. And the stories we're taught in school, from American folklore to Greek mythology, double down on the lesson. Paul Bunyan, anyone? How about John Henry and his hammer? Poor Sisyphus keeps pushing that rock up the hill, even though he knows it's going to roll right back down again. Every damned time.

Except in the case of consensus bad habits—smoking, using illegal narcotics, drinking alcohol to excess, overindulging in Nutter Butters—quitting isn't recommended. "Quitter" remains an insult, a mean jeer, a hurtful taunt that never loses its power to wound, even long after we've left the playgrounds of middle school. Quitting is granted a unique—and uniquely negative—spot in the pantheon of human behavior. It's set apart for special vilification. Rarely is it treated as an ordinary maneuver to be routinely deployed when a particular situation simply isn't working out.

The more I thought about it, the odder all of this seemed. Because for many people, both now and throughout history, quitting has proven to be a savvy strategy, as effective for *Homo sapiens* as it is for mice and birds. Reluctant as we may be to admit it, quitting *works*.

For a lot of us, our lives improve dramatically when we change direction, when we renounce current behaviors and embrace new ones. Without that willingness to stop and reconnoiter, we'd keep stumbling along in the same direction, even if the trip isn't taking us where we want to go, even if, in fact, it's making us downright miserable. Most of us can sense when we've reached that point and need to quit. So why don't we do it more often? And why, given its life-enhancing utility, does quitting have such an unsavory reputation?

To some people, the word "quit" sounds disgustingly weak. But its roots aren't nearly so negative. Etymology is a murky business, but one of the best guesses is that it comes to us from "quietare," the Latin verb for "to put to rest," and it has, like all words, evolved over time, picking up added definitional shadings from other languages and cultures. Dictionary.com provides three meanings: "to stop, cease, or discontinue"; "to depart from; leave"; and "to give up or resign; let go; relinquish." None of those words or phrases sounds meek to me. They sound decisive. Forward facing. Freeing.

———————

To get to the bottom of the business of quitting, I did what I've always done, not just as a journalist but as an incessantly curious (some might say "unrepentantly nosy and borderline annoying") human being. I put the question to almost everyone I know: *What's the most significant thing you've ever quit?* And then a follow-up: *Do you regret it?*

I pestered friends, family members, colleagues, neighbors, strangers in the Starbucks line, fellow dog owners at the dog park. And those people put me in touch with their friends and colleagues and family members, with people who have made all manner of shifts and changes in their lives, despite the cascade of earnest tips that heartily recommends the opposite, the life advice that is drilled into us from birth: *Keep on keepin' on! Winners never quit and quitters never win! Stay the course! Don't give up! You're not beaten until you quit!*

No one—not one person among the roughly 150 to whom I posed the Quitting Question—ever said, "No, sorry, I can't think of anything." *Everyone* had a Quitting Story. And they all wanted to talk about it. They were eager to join the conversation, demonstrating that the topic of giving up looms large in our lives. We profess to be ashamed of the times we've done it—and yet deep inside, we recognize the power of quitting to shake things up, to change us, to help us move forward. I loved hearing tales of how quitting has enabled people to stop what they're doing and strike out in new directions—sometimes with positive results, and sometimes not, because nothing in life is guaranteed, but always with hope for a better tomorrow. Many of those stories are included in this book.

Along the way, I did a deep dive into what I began to think of as the Curious World of the Quit. I began with the nuances of animal behavior, interviewing neuroscientists and evolutionary biologists and psychologists—the very researchers, that is, who are determined to solve the complex mystery of giving up: What happens in our brains when an action is abandoned? And then I expanded the circle of my inquiry, determined to find out everything about quitting that I could get my hands on, from self-help books to YouTube videos on the sunk-cost fallacy and opportunity cost to articles about the life coach fad and the choice architecture movement—because above all else, quitting is choosing.

Where, I wondered, do we get our convictions about quitting? Why do we avoid it so strenuously, and when we *do* manage to quit, why do we feel guilty about it?

Truth is, were it not for quitting, we'd have precious little scientific knowledge at all—because the increase of that knowledge requires the constant giving up of concepts that are superseded by new discoveries. Quitting is at the center of intellectual advancement. What if we refused to let go of an idea in the wake of updated information that proves it false? *Germs, scherms. Diseases are caused by evil spirits haunting the body. I've got a little pain right here— anybody know a good exorcist?*

Tim Birkhead, the British scientist whose books have made the world of birds wonderfully accessible, puts it this way: "When scientists retest someone else's ideas and find that evidence to be consistent with the original notion, then the idea remains. If, however, other researchers...find a better explanation for the facts, scientists can change their idea about what the truth is. Changing your mind in the light of new ideas or better evidence constitutes scientific progress."

Yet when it comes to our lives and the decisions we make about what to do next, quitting is still frowned upon, still labeled as the last refuge of the loser. Quitting may be marginally more acceptable today than in years past, thanks to a pandemic that made us question the point of joyless jobs and baleful bosses—but it's still not exactly a career enhancer. You don't often see "serial quitter" listed as a marketable skill on LinkedIn profiles.

The goal of this book, then, is not only to deliver the latest dispatches from the front lines of the science of giving up, but also to explore just how it is that we got suckered by the idea of grit in the first place. When and why did quitting become synonymous with failure? And in terms of the people who *do* quit, even in the face of cultural pressure to press on regardless, how were they able to pull it off? Their stories just might help you learn how to block out the hectoring media messages—and the bullying bullet points of too many self-help books—that preach perseverance as a can't-miss, never-fail strategy.

And while you may ultimately decide *not* to quit, the decision should be your own and not one based on somebody else's idea of what constitutes a brave and meaningful life.

So where *did* it all begin? How'd the idea that grit is virtuous and quitting is sinful ever get its hooks in us?

A major source, of course, is that nettlesome notion known as the Protestant work ethic. "Treating grit as a virtue is a relic of the Protestant Reformation," says Adam Grant, professor at the University of Pennsylvania's Wharton School and author of many bestselling books on personal transformation. It's "part of the American dream," he tells me.

And not just the American one. Other nations, too, put perseverance on a pedestal. If it weren't such an entrenched ideal, after all, then the recent mini backlash against it wouldn't be so newsworthy. As essayist Charlie Tyson observes, "From the 'lying flat' movement in China to outcries against deaths from overwork in Japan and South Korea, there is a growing sense of indignation in wealthy countries about inhumane work ideals." He adds Sweden and Finland to the list of countries who report surprising numbers of workers suffering from job-induced burnout—surprising because for so long, people just didn't quit, and the positive attributes of superhuman endurance were treated as truisms. Recently, the notion of lying flat took a more vigorous turn: "A new term," writes historian Rana Mitter, "has been seen on Chinese social media— *runxue*—the 'study of run,' as in 'running away.' Young Chinese workers are dispirited by the cocktail of Covid restrictions, highly competitive working environments and social pressures to get married and do well financially." Quitters, that is, are coming out of the closet. In a buzzed-about 2021 essay in the *New York Times*, Cassady

Rosenblum chronicles her journey from radio producer operating in "the cacophony of the 24-hour news cycle" to serene porch sitter: "Work has become intolerable. Rest is resistance."

Well, maybe. But it's not that simple, of course. Because if grit didn't still have such a powerful hold on our imaginations, we'd not be reading essays by people determined to reject it. "Suddenly talk of grit—being passionate about long-term goals, and showing the stamina to pursue them—seems to be everywhere," cognitive psychologist Daniel Willlingham wrote in 2016, as the perseverance movement began to gather even more cultural steam. And despite the temporary uptick in workers going AWOL, the traditional lessons of grit still linger: Quit and you'll fail. Keep your nose to the proverbial grindstone and you'll reap the rewards—even though it doesn't always end up that way in real life. Some people toil incessantly and go bankrupt, while others goof off and rake in the dough. Yet we're still primed to believe in the simple, cause-and-effect power of perseverance.

As you'll discover in this book, that glorification of grit has a dark side. The campaign against quitting has a checkered past, a complicated and even somewhat sinister history. There's a *reason* that quitting is so reviled—and that reason can be tracked down and interrogated. The celebration of perseverance as a surefire source of happiness and satisfaction didn't just happen; that veneration can be traced back to the place where it emerged from a thick tangle of culture and economics. Our positive attitudes toward grit have been deliberately cultivated. Grit is sold to us like cars and cornflakes and smartphones.

And that's a shame, because our lives can be transformed in positive ways when we quit, swapping out one destiny for another. If we decide that things need to change, quitting is the first step. (And that's true as well for the world as a whole. To ensure the planet's future, we know we must eventually quit fossil fuels and embrace creative and innovative new strategies for energy production.) Until we're able to stop in our tracks and rethink our lives, we may be stuck in a place where we don't really want to be.

Maybe you've known a few people like that—including yourself.

Perhaps you dealt with it by quitting your job. An unprecedented number of workers in the United States did just that over the past few years, as the pandemic forced us to reexamine our priorities. In the first eight months of 2021, 30 million Americans resigned from their jobs, the highest since the US Department of Labor began keeping track twenty years ago. Barely a week has gone by since 2020 that didn't feature a news story about someone turning in a company ID and a key card and saying merrily, "So long, suckers!"

The reason we hear those stories, however, is precisely *because* they're so unusual. The pandemic gave quitting a brief cachet—the phrase "the Great Resignation" has a high-minded grandeur to it—but let's face it. The general attitude toward quitting remains what it's always been: Something to avoid. Something in which only lazy losers indulge, as they snooze in front of a TV screen with a lapful of Cheez-It crumbs. Quitting still carries a stigma, a foul odor. If you quit your church, your yoga class, your political party, your plant-based diet, or your marriage, you'll still be judged. Quitting something will still provoke a swift reaction from your friends and maybe your mother—maybe especially your mother: "What were you *thinking*? Did you really give it a fair shot? Did you even *try*?" We've all heard the old saw: Don't quit a job (or a love affair) until you've got another one lined up, ready to go.

We're still informed on a regular basis—via podcasts and moms—that quitting is proof of a weak character, of a lack of initiative and follow-through. Quitting means you'll never succeed, never amount to anything. (Many of the people I interviewed for this book were happy to talk about resigning from a job, getting a divorce, or changing course in any one of a dozen different ways, but they bristled at the *q* word. *I didn't quit,* they'd say in a huff. *I just left one situation for another, okay?* Um, okay.)

Perseverance, by contrast, still sports that sparkling reputation. It's earnestly praised in the aforesaid podcasts and manifold motivational speeches, in an infinite reel of YouTube lecturettes and an eternity's worth of TED Talks, the kind that get millions of views. Slogans that extol it are emblazoned on workout gear. Self-help is a robust worldwide business, earning an estimated $11 billion annually. Books that recommend grit are bestsellers, as they declare with gusto that doggedness is good and quitting is bad. *Very* bad. Your future, these manifestos maintain, is totally in your own hands. If you work hard and follow a rigorous plan—and most of all, *if you do not quit*—you win. If you give up, though, you fail. Furthermore, you *deserve* to.

Quitting is presented as an extremity. A last resort. A point of no return. Indulge in it too many times and you'll be known as a failure, a flake, a wastrel, a spineless wimp—even though it might be exactly what you need to do. The disconnect between quitting's benefits and its bad reputation can be jarring. It's no wonder that quitting takes up an enormous amount of space in our psyches—both individually and collectively—and influences how we see ourselves and our world. Quitting may *feel* right, but it *looks* wrong.

Even the famous feel the sting.

Scottie Pippen is a champion. Yet despite everything he accomplished in a spectacular seventeen-year career spent mostly with the Chicago Bulls, the former NBA star was tagged once and apparently forever with an odious nickname: "Quittin' Pippen." During interviews to promote his 2021 memoir, *Unguarded*, he was pestered repeatedly about a single incident *from almost three decades ago*—demonstrating that our umbrage at the idea of quitting apparently has no expiration date.

It happened in game three in the 1994 semifinals of the NBA playoffs. The opponent was the New York Knicks. With 1.8 seconds left in a tied game, Pippen refused to go back on the court after a time-out because Bulls coach Phil Jackson had tapped Toni Kukoc to take the final shot. Miffed at the snub, Pippen sat and sulked. (Kukoc hit the shot to win the game, which probably didn't help Pippen's mood.) Pippen has been known henceforth not as the superlative athlete he is but as a quitter.

And even when the world is more sympathetic to a famous athlete's decision to quit, it still feels entitled to judge. Ash Barty was the number one tennis player in the world when she suddenly gave up the sport in early 2022 at age twenty-five. Columnist Emma Kemp praised the Australian for the gutsy move but noted, "Not a soul outside her inner circle saw this coming." Barty's announcement on Instagram had a defensive ring, as if she were getting ready to block shots before they even crossed the net: "I just know that I am absolutely—I am spent—I just know that physically I have nothing more to give."

A few months earlier, in the "I quit" heard around the world, Simone Biles withdrew from the 2021 Olympics, citing mental health concerns. Granted, many people on Twitter and other platforms professed support for her, but those you-go-girl comments were deployed because so many *other* people—including Piers Morgan, the acerbic British TV host—snarled the opposite: that by quitting, Biles was being unpatriotic and selfish. She was letting down her country and her team. And squandering her astonishing talent.

We'll return to Biles and her remarkably courageous move in

chapter 1, but for now, let's focus on how the decision to quit forever alters one's public image. No matter what happens to Biles or to Barty in the future, it will be *the* question they face in every interview: Not "How'd you get to be such a great athlete?" but "Why'd you quit?"

Andrew Luck can relate. He left football fans flummoxed—and provoked some less-than-flattering comments in that bloodthirsty arena known as sports talk radio—when he abruptly abandoned a career as a top NFL quarterback in 2019. Before Luck, legendary athletes Sandy Koufax, Barry Sanders, and Björn Borg abandoned their careers long before their skills had diminished to the point where they'd no longer be able to compete. (If you're a professional athlete, they call it "retirement" even if you're only twenty-nine, as Luck was when he left.) At their level of fame and accomplishment, giving up is a cataclysmic decision. It means they must remake themselves, top to bottom: "Quitting was an act of imagination and emancipation," Koufax biographer Jane Leavy wrote of the ace lefty's decision to walk away from Major League Baseball. "It required the ability to conceive of an existence as full and as important as the one he had so publicly led."

Greta Garbo is known these days as much for quitting Hollywood in her prime as she is for her acting. Composer Jean Sibelius? He created ravishingly beautiful symphonies and chill-down-your-spine violin concertos—but stopped writing music seriously at sixty-two, three decades before his death. The silence of Dashiell Hammett after publishing *The Maltese Falcon* and other crime fiction masterpieces is a greater mystery than any he crafted in his work: Why did he put away his pen forever?

When Prince Harry and Meghan Markle said goodbye to Buckingham Palace, relinquishing membership in the British royal family, public outrage was swift and furious: They can't just *quit*, can they?

They could. They did. And the world watched, agog.

We watched because we're intrigued by quitting, fascinated by it, maybe even a little obsessed by it, and at the same time we're leery of it. Quitting is forbidden fruit. It challenges our most fundamental beliefs about how the world works, about what we want—for ourselves and for the people we care about—and what we can do to get it. People disagree every day about the best way to raise children, for instance, but almost nobody questions the importance of teaching them to persevere. As Lindsay Crouse wrote in a *New York Times* essay in 2021, "Americans often demonize quitting and valorize 'grit'—a mythical quality that a flurry of books urged parents to instill in children over the last decade." Refusing to quit is held up as heroic. "Hard work is likely the most universally cherished American value," noted Charlie Tyson, adding, "One recent Pew survey found that 80 percent of Americans describe themselves as 'hardworking'—outstripping all other traits. Work has gotten worse, yet our work ideals remain elevated." Quitting doesn't fit the dominant view of how success is achieved. It's a perverse aberration, a grubby little outlier. Far better to stick with a lousy, soul-killing gig than to ditch it for the dream of something better—because if you leave, you'll be labeled a quitter before you're halfway out the door.

Most of us will never find ourselves performing a double backflip with a triple twist in a floor exercise in front of millions of TV viewers. (I get the twisties just thinking about it.) We'll never be called upon to lead an NFL or NBA team to victory, as Luck and Pippen did, or compose a symphony, or win Wimbledon, or strike out the side, or represent the British monarchy.

But we all face moments when the question of quitting—should I or shouldn't I?—preoccupies us. Amy Dickinson, author of the advice column *Ask Amy*, tells me that quitting is, hands down, the number one reason people write to her seeking help with their problems: "Honestly, I think the idea of quitting pervades the questions sent to me, whether it's quitting a marriage, a friendship, a habit or an obligation," she says. "The flip side of this, of course, is the pain of being dropped, abandoned, neglected—the pain of having someone quit *you*."

It's no mystery, then, why a lot of us seek outside help—from an advice columnist or a dad—to deal with this dilemma, this perpetual puzzle: quitting doesn't feel like a viable option. Yet when a course of action isn't working, we feel an instinctual pull to change it. Our deepest drives tell us to do what we need to do in order to survive, including giving up and trying something else. But we get a powerful countermessage from the outside world. Social conditioning kicks in, and we question those drives, the ones telling us to bail. There's often a sharp disparity between our robust internal conviction—*I have to get out of here RIGHT NOW*—and the signals sent forth by chatty best friends, well-meaning parents, and the authors of self-help books: If you quit, you're letting everyone down. Especially yourself.

In some ways, we *overthink* the issue of giving up, searching for complex reasons for what can, after all, be boiled down to a simple binary choice: Quit or keep going? In other ways, we seriously *underthink* it. Because quitting is something we do, yes, but it's also an idea—an idea about the world and what shapes it, and about our responsibilities to ourselves and to others. And about how to be happy.

To be clear, quitting is not always the right thing to do. Along with historic levels of people leaving jobs during the pandemic, a record number of college students dropped out. More than a quarter of all students who started classes at four-year American universities in the fall of 2019 didn't return the next year, an increase of two percentage points over the previous year and the highest dropout rate since 2012. Among community college students, 3.5 percent didn't come back in 2020. No one would argue that less education is a positive.

Moreover, perseverance is not inherently a bad thing. You need resilience to get through life's inevitable challenges and travails. But making grit the go-to solution for every dilemma—and looking down on people who fail to exhibit it—can lead to some unfortunate outcomes, such as blaming yourself for things that are outside your control. Or blaming others for things that they can't control, either. Quitting is not the simple on-off switch that we've been led to believe it is. It's a complex intellectual and emotional feat—which is why scientists are increasingly curious about how our brains pull it off.

Thanks to a recent series of breakthroughs in neuroscience labs around the world, we're on the cusp of understanding as never before the means by which living entities give up when an action doesn't seem to be advantageous. These discoveries hold the promise of helping with the other kind of quitting, too—the kind we indisputably want to encourage: breaking the grip of addiction to drugs, alcohol, and excessive eating, as well as relieving the suffering caused by conditions such as obsessive-compulsive disorder and clinical depression.

In the pages that follow, we'll meet the researchers who devise ingenious experiments to find out how organisms such as zebrafish, honeybees, rats, finches, crows, and bowerbirds quit. And then we'll circle back around to creatures who live a little closer to home: people. We'll consider the high cost of refusing to give up when a once-promising new product or business is clearly a bust. (Here's looking at *you*, Theranos and WeWork.) We'll figure out how to deal with the fact that when you quit something, you may very well hurt and disappoint the people you love, from parents and partners and friends to bosses and mentors. And we'll reflect upon how often quitting shows up as a theme in popular culture, from a pugnacious country ballad like "Take This Job and Shove It" to a literary work like *Moby-Dick* to an iconic movie like *Jerry Maguire* to a TV series like *Hacks*. We'll ponder why quitting scenes energize so many of our most cherished stories—and how we can use our responses to those moments to better understand ourselves.

We'll ruminate on the major role played by luck and probability in our lives, even though we don't much like to acknowledge it— because we prefer to believe we're calling the shots. Trains jump tracks, planes crash, people who lead healthy lifestyles come down with terrible diseases. Conversely, a randomly selected Powerball number pays off or you meet the love of your life in the license-renewal line at the DMV. We're dealt a good hand or a bad one, and many times success or failure isn't a matter of perseverance—but a roll of the dice. Pure chance. So why do some of the most famous and influential self-help books ever published, longtime bestsellers by authors such as Napoleon Hill and Norman Vincent Peale, insist that our destiny is completely up to us? Why is that message so appealing—and so dangerous? We'll peek behind the platitudes and find out.

And we'll see how other people manage to make giving up a creative act, the launch pad for the rest of their lives. Throughout the book are White Flag Moments: first-person accounts by people who quit when they had to. Sometimes it's the people who shared their Quitting Story with me for this book, and sometimes it's celebrities who have written about the specific point when they gave up in order to get what they really wanted. Each brief testimony records the instant when someone—maybe someone whose dilemma sounds a lot like one you've faced, too—realized that it was time to pause. Time to take a breath. Time to reassess. Time to quit.

As you read about these epiphanies, you may be inspired to review the watershed moments in your own history, the hinge points upon which a life turns—so that when they come around again, you'll be ready to act. That might mean quitting. Or it might not. But whatever you decide, it will be *you* who does the deciding, based upon the circumstances of your life, and not upon some remote, abstract, one-size-fits-all ideal of perseverance.

At the end of each chapter, you'll find nudges for next steps called Permission Slips. These suggestions may help you as you consider the wisdom of strategic quitting. Because sooner or later, you'll face the Quitting Question.

Not that you haven't faced it before. We all have. Everybody has a Quitting List, a compendium of jobs or relationships or pastimes or belief systems or ways of being in the world that needed to be relinquished. Mine started with that excruciating moment in Morgantown, but it didn't end there. It happened again a few years later, during my first newspaper job in Ashland, Kentucky. Despite racking up A-plus performance reviews, I discovered that I was making one-fourth—*one-fourth!*—the salary of the man who'd held the job before me. When I asked for an explanation, the managing editor was surprised by my inquiry: *Why, Stan's a man with a family, Julia. And you're a twenty-one-year-old single woman.* Case closed.

He wouldn't budge. So I quit. Granted, it was only fractionally easier the second time around. And afterward, another towel was drenched during another dark night of the soul. (*What's going to* happen *to me? I was a fool! No, I wasn't. Yes, I was!*) Somehow, I muddled through.

Giving up that job could've turned out to be a catastrophe. As I said before—and it's important enough to repeat—the embrace of quitting as a life strategy doesn't mean that things will always work out. They won't. It only means that you get to be in charge of your own life—even in the face of a fear of making the wrong choice. In the end, there's really no such thing as a wrong choice. The only true error is to make no choice at all. Because somebody else will be more than happy to make it for you.

Among the people I interviewed about giving up, from scientists and scholars and historians to regular folks like you and me, one thing was true across the board: people generally have more regrets about the times they *should* have quit but didn't than about the times when they did.

————

So what will this book do for you? You can think of it, perhaps, as a DIY quit kit, like an item you'd tote home from IKEA—only in this case, you'll be snapping together a little something to upgrade your life instead of just your living room. You'll have a new way to think about quitting. A new context for making decisions about the things you care about, from your family and your work to your well-being. A fresh angle on gumption and perseverance.

If nothing else, I hope this book persuades you to at least consider the possibility that grit—or the lack thereof—isn't the only way to assess a life. I hope it gives you the freedom to *not* be obsessively dedicated and self-reliant.

To *not* always overcome obstacles.

To *not* finish everything you start.

If you let yourself quit when you're compelled to, you expand the possibilities for your life. You prove that you believe in abundance—because quitting is about hope. Quitting is about tomorrow. Quitting is about the capacity to change, again and again, as often as you're compelled to do so.

The secret of a joyful and productive life may well reside not in those qualities we're often told are the key ones—doggedness and resolve—but in nimbleness. In flexibility. In the load-lightening act of giving up, an act that precedes a daring jump into the future. In the glorious and gutsy embrace of a new way of being.

In knowing when to quit.

Because quitting is an act of love.

PART I

QUITTING:
IT'S ALL IN YOUR HEAD

There's a point at which perseverance
becomes denial.

—*Benjamin Wood*

Chapter One

What Birds, Bees, and Gymnasts Can Teach Us about Giving Up

Misguided grit is the worst possible quality a person can have.

—John A. List

How is Simone Biles like a honeybee?

That's not a riddle. Nor is it a trick question. It's a profoundly serious inquiry, and the answer is found within an emerging field of neuroscience, one that promises to unlock the secrets of how our brains decide if it's the right time to quit.

As the world's premier gymnast, Biles has done many amazing things, but it was the thing she did in Tokyo in 2021 that stunned the world like nothing else in her career ever had: she gave up.

So what's the connection between one of the greatest athletes in history and a flying insect?

Stick around. We'll get to that shortly.

———

"Perseverance, in a biological sense, doesn't make sense unless it's *working.*"

That's Jerry Coyne, emeritus professor at the University of Chi-cago, one of the top evolutionary biologists of his generation. I've called Coyne to ask him about animals and quitting. I want to know why human beings tend to adhere to the Gospel of Grit—while other creatures on this magnificently diverse earth of ours follow a different strategy. Their lives are marked by purposeful halts, for-tuitous side steps, canny retreats, nick-of-time recalculations, wily work-arounds, and deliberate do-overs, not to mention loops, pivots, and complete reversals.

Other animals, that is, quit on a regular basis. And they don't obsess about it, either.

I catch up with Coyne on a Sunday morning just before he goes out for his twice-daily ritual: feeding the ducks in the body of water near the center of campus called Botany Pond. His office overlooks the pond, where some two dozen ducklings hatch each spring. Coyne officially retired in 2015 but still goes into his office every day to work. When Covid-19 shut down the university in 2020, he was granted a special waiver to come and feed the ducks. He keeps up the habit because he enjoys it. Ditto for the ducks.

In the wild, Coyne points out, perseverance has no special status. Animals do what they do because it furthers their agenda: to last long enough to reproduce, ensuring the continuation of their genetic material.

We're animals, too, of course. And despite all the complex wonders that human beings have created—from Audis to alge-bra, from hot-fudge sundaes to haiku, from suspension bridges to *Bridgerton*—at bottom our instincts are always goading us toward the same basic, no-nonsense goal: to stick around so that we can pass along little copies of ourselves. It's axiomatic: the best way to survive is to give up on whatever's not contributing to survival. To waste as few resources as possible on the ineffective. "Human behavior has been molded to help us obtain a favorable outcome," Coyne tells me. We go for what works. We're biased toward results.

Yet somewhere between the impulse to follow what strikes us as the most promising path—which means quitting an *un*promising path—and the simple act of giving up, something often gets in the way. And that's the mystery that intrigues me: When quitting is the right thing to do, why don't we always do it?

Consider the finches on the Galápagos Islands, the place that fired the imagination of the young Charles Darwin in 1835 and led to his great breakthrough: the theory of natural selection. A finch's diet on the island consists mainly of small seeds, some of which are contained inside a sharp-spined weed called a caltrop. Finches use their beaks to remove the seeds from that sheath. And it's not easy.

As Jonathan Weiner explains in his Pulitzer Prize–winning book, *The Beak of the Finch*, a persevering finch is a doomed finch. If birds spend too long pecking away at a caltrop with an especially tough hide, they're in big trouble. "When times are hard," Weiner writes, "their lives depend on how efficiently they can forage for food—how little energy they can expend in getting how much energy in return." The finches that know when to give up and move on to another potential food source have a better chance of survival, because they're not depleting themselves in a quest with diminishing nutritional returns.

Some finches, Weiner writes, lavish up to six minutes on the exasperating task of digging out a single seed. "That's a long time for a bird to struggle, and most of the time the bird just gives up after a while." A finch gets it: if at first you don't succeed, quit. Struggle is nature's way of hinting that it's better to move along to more promising mealtime possibilities. If staying alive is the goal, then a task without a quick payoff in the survival sweepstakes is best abandoned. A finch with grit could soon be a deceased one.

Nature has a knack for cutting to the chase. There are no medals or accolades on the line. This is a no-frills zone. Actions can't be superfluous—they *matter*. The organism's very existence is at stake. Quitting is a skill, a survival technique. It's not—as we humans sometimes treat it—a moral failing. And resisting the impulse to quit isn't necessarily brave or noble. It's nonsensical.

Unlike humans, those other creatures aren't burdened by some abstract idea of the benefits of perseverance. When a behavior isn't getting them anywhere—or when it's proving to be perilous to their continued existence—they stop.

In his marvelous book *Entangled Life: How Fungi Make Our Worlds, Change Our Minds & Shape Our Futures*, Merlin Sheldrake makes a surprising point about slime molds. These organisms may lack a central nervous system and rely instead upon "exploratory networks made of tentacle-like veins," but "they can still 'make decisions.'" They do this, he writes, by stopping and then going in another direction. Observed in a petri dish by a team of Japanese scientists, slime molds "compared a range of possible courses of action and can find the shortest point between two points in a labyrinth."

Slime molds don't like bright light, and so at the point where researchers placed a light, the organisms quickly changed course. If one road wasn't right, slime molds gave up on it and chose another. Pursuing an undesirable path because it's the gritty thing to do makes no sense—not even for slime mold.

As Coyne writes in the opening passages of *Why Evolution Is True*, "Plants and animals seem intricately and almost perfectly designed for living their lives. Squids and flatfish change color and pattern to blend in with their surroundings, becoming invisible to predator and prey. Bats have radar to home in on insects at night.

Hummingbirds, which can hover in place and change position in an instant, are far more agile than any human helicopter." And if need be, they quit.

―――――――

Among the experiments designed to test the cognitive abilities of birds, tests described by Jennifer Ackerman in her revelatory book *The Genius of Birds*, is one conducted by McGill University biologist Louis Lefebvre.

He and his team at a research station on Barbados placed edible seeds in two cups, one green and one yellow. They observed individual bullfinches and grackles to see which birds were attracted to which cup color. Once that was established, researchers switched out the loose seeds in the cup of the preferred color for seeds that they glued to the bottom of the cup. No matter how hard the bird tried, she wouldn't be able to remove the glued-on seeds.

Lefebvre and his colleagues watched to see how long it would take a bird to give up on the glued-on seeds in the cup of her favorite color and then, when she was stymied, to try the other cup—which contained seeds *not* glued on. The birds caught on fairly quickly, moving from a futile task to one with a payoff. Dealing with preferred color was nice—but it's nothing compared to dinner.

The experiment was designed to measure the birds' "flexible thinking," Ackerman writes. But it seems to me that it demonstrates a corollary principle as well: the utility of quitting. At a basic level, quitting boils down to ceasing one action in order to initiate another. Quitting, then, is an integral link in the chain of a bird's cognitive steps. Unless she is willing to give up on procuring the seed that is, unbeknownst to her, forever inaccessible even though it's tantalizingly visible in the favored cup, she goes hungry. Grit for its own sake is irrelevant to a bird. Survival, not style points, is the goal. And in this case, quitting and moving on is the only effective strategy for the bird to get a meal.

We have to be cautious, of course, about concocting neat parallels between the animal world and our own, and ascribing too many human qualities to animals whose thoughts and emotions are, after all, unknown to us. As Sheldrake, the fungus fancier, writes, "The prevailing scientific view is that it is a mistake to imagine that there is anything deliberate about most nonhuman interactions." But it's hard to resist seeing links here and there, as we observe other creatures' decisions to quit when it benefits them.

 WHITE FLAG MOMENT

Here's how I imagined my resignation: I would wait for that familiar feeling to set in, the one in which I'd sooner be swallowed into the Earth's core than complete one more work task. Then, instead of doing it, I'd simply...not. I would not answer the email...I'd tell my editor, "You know what, actually? Today's my last day." Then I'd sign out of Slack, forever.

—*Katie Heaney*

In a research facility in New Zealand, Ackerman writes, a scientist named Alex Taylor tried to figure out how a crow thinks. He and his assistants set up a play area for crows in which, if the crow lifts a stick, the stick pulls a string; the string is attached to a chunk of meat. Ergo, the crow gets a snack. If the crow is able to see the snack coming his way, the lifting and the pulling happen with no hesitation. If, however, the crow's view of the meat is blocked, the crow stops trying. Perseverance is linked to the assurance of a tangible reward. And so it makes sense.

"Without the visual reinforcement of meat moving closer and closer, cuing them to keep up the activity," Ackerman explains in her book, "only one crow out of eleven spontaneously pulled the string a sufficient number of times to get the meat." Crows "have an extraordinary ability to notice the consequences of their actions." If they believe an activity's not getting them anywhere, they stop doing it. Requiring sustenance, as all living creatures do, a crow can't waste her efforts on a less-than-sure thing. She makes a calculation, balancing the probable expenditure of energy and time against the potential for a food payday: *I'm hungry. Any chow in sight, justifying a bunch of tugs on this silly little string? No? See you later.*

Let's take a quick moment to imagine if the experiment were done with humans instead of crows. Influenced by our valorization of grit, we'd be tempted to whoop and cheer for number eleven, the one who kept at it even with no guarantees that her effort was worthwhile: *You go, girl! Don't give up!* We'd call the other ten quitters. Yet the reality is that putting forth effort on behalf of a goal that might not pan out can sap resources better directed elsewhere. Birds live on a much thinner margin of survival than do humans, of course, but the lesson holds for both: perseverance isn't always the best strategy.

A similar cost-to-benefit ratio was observed in decisions made by male bowerbirds, the boy toys of the bird world. They "don't offer any direct benefits as helpmates" to female bowerbirds, Ackerman writes. It's all about a superficial show of looking flashy and appealing. The males engage in flamboyant dances and frenzied wing flicks, in loud squeaks and lively hopping—all to attract potential mates. The showstopper is an elaborate construction project: the odd little grotto that a male bowerbird creates out of bits and bobs and sticks and shiny trinkets—anything that can be easily scavenged—to impress females of the species.

Male bowerbirds love to hoard blue items. Researchers don't know why, but there you are: Blue rules. Red items, though, are shunned. If a male bowerbird finds a red object in his stash, he'll quickly remove it from the nest and testily discard it. Thus, to gauge the problem-solving capacity of a bowerbird, researchers placed a red tile in the bower, securing it to the ground with screws, impossible for the bird to remove.

Digging and scratching and tugging at the hated red tile, trying to dislodge it, proves to be pointless. At some point, the bowerbird gets it. "The cleverer males," Ackerman writes, "quickly discovered a novel strategy to deal with the situation—cover up the red with leaf litter or other decorations."

Before they can deploy plan B, however, these Einsteins of the bowerbird world must complete one essential step: they have to dump plan A. They must stop digging and scratching. They have to abandon the scheme that *isn't* working and come up with one that might. In other words, they have to quit. Otherwise, they won't be able to attract a mate and thereby pass along their genes.

Nature is ruthlessly efficient: all business, all the time. "The more one learns about plants and animals," Coyne has written, "the more one marvels about how their designs fit their way of life." They must obtain a maximum rate of return in sustenance for their outlay of effort—or they perish. It's a coldly unforgiving ratio. Every gesture, every decision, must sync up with the goal of survival.

Which brings us back to the Biles and the bees.

———————

The finals of the 2021 Tokyo Olympics wasn't the first time Biles withdrew from a competition. It happened in 2013, at an event in the United States, and at least two other times, too, just as it does for other gymnasts. And while sportswriters have tried, at one time or another during Biles's spectacular career, to explain what makes her so special—is it her uncanny balance, her extraordinary focus and poise, her stunning flexibility, her immense core strength, the iron rigor of her training ritual, or as Biles herself speculated to *New York* in 2021, the gift of "a God-given talent"?—the truly essential element might be none of the above.

All of those attributes are important, yes. But what if the most important one is the ability to quit strategically when the price of *not* quitting is too high?

That notion goes against virtually everything we're taught to believe about the resiliency of champions, about their nonstop drive and relentless sense of purpose. But maybe resilience can mean more than just overcoming obstacles, more than just clenching your fists and ignoring pain and powering your way through.

Maybe resilience—paradoxically—can also mean the willingness to quit.

At that moment in Tokyo, Biles made a swift, critical assessment: *Is this worth what I'm risking?* "I was not physically capable," she later told *New York*'s Camonghne Felix. She hadn't felt her usual surge of confidence when she'd arrived in the country five days earlier, she recalled, and her doubts had only intensified as the preliminary events went on.

Her sport is one that involves split-second timing and the perpetual risk of severe injury. Not being able to locate your body in space—the aptly named "twisties"—is terrifying, Biles noted, and the stakes could not be higher: "It's basically life or death."

For elite athletes like Biles, an understanding of their physical capacity is at the center of everything they undertake. They must be aware, second by second, with pinpoint precision, of their strengths and weaknesses. Thus, for an athlete as in tune with her body as Biles is, the choice was clear. For all the satisfaction that her sport brings her, all the exhilaration, and all that was riding on her participation that day, it wasn't worth the risk of death or catastrophic injury. The heroic choice, the resilient choice, was not the choice to persevere. It was the choice to quit.

Unlike a honeybee, Biles can't fly (although if you've seen her in action, you know she comes a lot closer than the rest of us ever will). But she *does* share an important trait with honeybees that may have contributed to her remarkable rise: understanding when to quit.

––––––––––

Justin O. Schmidt is a renowned entomologist and author of *The Sting of the Wild*, a nifty book about a nasty thing: stinging insects. Living creatures, he tells me, echoing Coyne, have two goals, and those goals are rock-bottom rudimentary: "To eat and not be eaten." If something's not working, an animal stops doing it—and with a notable absence of fuss or excuse-making.

Human beings are the only creatures who quit and then stew over it, writing self-flagellating social media posts, confessing doubts to friends over cocktails, calling ourselves names as we stare mournfully in the mirror.

For a honeybee, the drive to survive carries within it the commitment to make sure there will be more honeybees. And so she defends her colony with reckless abandon. When a honeybee stings a potential predator, she dies, because the sting eviscerates her. (Only the females sting.) Given those odds—a 100 percent mortality rate after stinging—what honeybee in her right mind would make the decision to sting if it didn't bring some benefit?

That's why, Schmidt explains to me from his lab in Tucson, sometimes she stands down. When a creature that may pose a threat approaches the colony, the honeybee might very well *not* sting. She chooses, in effect, to quit—to not take the next step and rush forward to defend the nest, at the cost of her life.

His experiments, the results of which he published in 2020 in *Insectes Sociaux*, an international scientific journal focusing on social insects such as bees, ants, and wasps, reveal that honeybees make a calculation on the fly, as it were. They decide if a predator is close enough to the colony to be a legitimate threat and, further, if the colony has enough reproductive potential at that point to warrant her ultimate sacrifice. If the moment meets those criteria—genuine peril (*check*), fertile colony (*check*)—the honeybees are fierce fighters, happy to perish for the greater good.

But if not…well, no. They don't engage. "Bees must make life-or-death decisions based on risk-benefit evaluations," Schmidt tells me. Like a gymnast facing a dizzyingly difficult maneuver that could prove to be lethal, they weigh the danger of their next move against what's at stake, measuring the imminent peril against the chances of success and the potential reward. They calculate odds. And if the ratio doesn't make sense, they quit.

So quitting might save your life if you're a finch or a honeybee—or an Olympic athlete. But what about the rest of us?

We don't usually perish when we tell someone who's getting in our personal space to scram—as a honeybee does a predator. Or when we spend too many minutes trying to peel the foil wrap from a Chipotle burrito, which is perhaps the closest human equivalent to a finch with an uncooperative caltrop. Can quitting be a matter of life or death for us as well?

Tragically, the answer is yes.

In 2001, a Northwestern University football player named

Rashidi Wheeler died during an August practice session. That same year, a player for the Minnesota Vikings, Korey Stringer, also died after a vigorous workout in extremely hot conditions. In 2018, an athlete at the University of Maryland, Jordan McNair, collapsed and later died of heat stroke after pushing himself relentlessly in practice on a sweltering day. And in 2020, Grant Brace, a wrestler at the University of the Cumberlands, died during a team drill that required players to run up and down a hill on a hot day. According to news accounts, Brace said, "I need water. Somebody help me. I feel like I am going to die." Between 1998 and 2018, at least thirty-four athletes died during practices.

These bright, able individuals had to have been aware that something was wrong. The symptoms of heat exhaustion aren't subtle: dizziness, severe headache, nausea, slurred speech, muscle cramping. But they didn't stop. They overrode their body's signals to quit. And the people around them who presumably weren't impaired—coaches and teammates—allegedly didn't tell them to. How could intelligent people and their conscientious mentors miss the signs?

 WHITE FLAG MOMENT

I didn't want to give up [during a competitive long-distance swim]. It was so strange. I could feel myself slipping away... There was something so awful in giving up. But...I just let go of myself. I let my face fall into the water, felt myself being dragged toward the boat. I was choking on that thick water, and then they were lifting me into the boat...Everything hurt so much...With utter exasperation the doctor said, "Doesn't she realize she was in a life-threatening situation?"

—Lynne Cox

Our bodies, after all, are *designed* to tell us when to quit. They go on high alert when we put them under intense stress. They send us messages to stop, and those messages come with the equivalent of a yelping siren and a flashing red light. As Stanford University professor Robert Sapolsky writes in his classic book on the physiology of stress, *Why Zebras Don't Get Ulcers*, our bodies try their damnedest to let us know when we're overloaded and can't maintain allostatic equilibrium: heart rate, breathing rate, and blood pressure all shoot up. *We're in trouble here*, our bodies scream at us. *Mayday. Mayday.*

Importantly, this distress isn't just physical. Psychological stress can be equally acute and have similarly dire consequences if ignored. As Bessel van der Kolk puts it in his humane and distinguished book *The Body Keeps the Score: Brain, Mind, and Body in the Healing of Trauma*, "The most important job of the brain is to ensure our survival, even under the most miserable conditions. Everything else is secondary."

If our lives have somehow gotten away from us, if we're not doing what feels right, if we're not nourishing our bodies and our souls properly, if we don't live according to the values and standards we once envisioned for ourselves, the impact on our overall well-being can be catastrophic. If we don't quit, we may not survive.

Just ask Jody Alyn.

———

"When I decided to get a divorce, my friends said, 'Why are you doing that?' I said, 'Because I'm dying.' Internally, emotionally— that's how it felt," Alyn tells me. "I actually said to people, 'I got out before I died.'"

She worked at a mental health center for many years and also served as diversity coordinator for the city of Colorado Springs. After that, she opened a consulting firm for businesses and individuals. It's still going strong. She's funny, smart, articulate, and engaging. She's thoughtful and measured.

She is not, in other words, someone who commonly indulges in hyperbole. Or lets her emotions get out of hand.

Yet when she describes to me her reasons for ending her marriage after raising two kids, and for completely upending her life, Alyn presents the decision in the kind of starkly dramatic terms that a hungry finch would understand: if she didn't quit, she'd perish.

Alyn wasn't the only one who framed her choice that way. Throughout dozens of interviews, other people made the same point. In fact, there was a remarkable similarity to the way people talked to me about their decision to change significant aspects of their lives. The stories all had different details, but one phrase showed up across the board: life or death.

They didn't see quitting as one more option among many options. Quitting, they say, felt like *life itself.* Many were emphatic about that: Quitting is not just a good idea. It's oxygen. It's basic sustenance.

"In my training, I'd learned a high degree of perseverance," Alyn tells me. "I could get through anything. I could turn challenges into 'learning experiences,'" she says, pronouncing the words with wry irony. "But the truth is, I stayed in situations longer than I should. I have to be in a lot of pain before I know it's time to make a change."

Her friends didn't understand just how much she was ailing, Alyn recalls, even when she tried to confide in them. "I got that all the time—'You look fine!' But what it looks like from the outside and what it feels like on the inside are two *entirely* different things. I finally just thought to myself, 'I can't stand it anymore.'"

On September 4, 2021, she packed up her gray Subaru Outback and drove out of Colorado Springs, heading east. "I had this idea— I'd take a year and live in different places and I'd figure out where I wanted to live. If I had to work in a coffee shop or a bookstore or a library or wherever, I would."

So how's it working out? "It's been fabulous. I can't tell you how magnificent it's been. I have not had one moment of regret."

She admits that it was hard at first to get used to the idea of just...*giving up*. And starting again. "Oh, it's such a slur—'Quitter!' My father used to say, 'You've got to have stick-to-itiveness.' And 'If a job is once begun, never leave it till it's done.' Something about the Protestant work ethic seeps into us the same way implicit bias always does. And when we change course, there's an element of having been wrong—of having made a mistake." Which is not an especially pleasant thing to acknowledge.

When I ask her if she feels courageous for having made such a dramatic change, Alyn quickly demurs: "Is it courageous to say, 'I'm not going to let myself die?' No. It's not courage. It's self-preservation." Then she offers a warm, knowing laugh. "An important part of a 'Fuck it—I'm *doing* this' moment is that you don't have to justify everything you're doing. You really only have one life."

———————

A similar epiphany came to Christine Sneed, a writer and teacher who worked in Chicago for two decades until the moment in May 2018 when she suddenly realized that her life felt all wrong to her.

"I had to leave. I couldn't keep doing the same things I was doing," she tells me, despite the fact that those "things" included a solid record of accomplishment. She'd published four well-reviewed books in six years while teaching writing at Northwestern University. But she felt stuck. Directionless. "It was a matter of being able to get out of bed in the morning with the same appetite. I was so tired all the time. I just had to trust my instincts."

So she and her partner, Adam, a youth soccer coach, moved to Pasadena, California. She's writing screenplays in addition to novels now. "Even if it's hard—it's *my* life. I don't regret the choices I've made. Being here has felt like a renewal. Back in Chicago, I felt I couldn't look down on the valley below our condo anymore without strangling myself." Archly, she adds, "Or someone else!"

For both women, and for other people you'll meet in this book, the growing conviction that they absolutely had to make a significant change in their lives wasn't a fleeting impulse, a casual "Well, maybe *someday*..." sort of idle contemplation. It was a radical, now-or-never step. A threshold. A portal into a new world.

———

Human brains, like the brains of all living creatures, know what to do when survival is on the line: quit and do something else. Alyn's brain knew. Sneed's knew. Even slime mold in a petri dish knows. So why don't more of us do it on a regular basis?

In their provocative book *Burnout: The Secret to Unlocking the Stress Cycle*, Emily Nagoski and Amelia Nagoski note that knowing when to quit "comes to us the same way it comes to the bird and the squirrel—in a quiet intuition that is outside rationality. We simply hear the voice inside us saying, 'You've done all you can here. It's time to move on.'" Too often, though, we tune it out: "Humans—especially women—have an extraordinary capacity to ignore this voice."

Women in abusive relationships are sometimes counseled by well-meaning friends and family members to forgive a perpetrator and try again, to avoid breaking up a home. They're advised that commitment to an intimate partner should take precedence over everything—including physical or emotional harm inflicted by that person.

To give up and get out—to quit a relationship—is to challenge powerful social norms, the Nagoski sisters write: "We live in a culture that values 'self-control,' 'grit,' and persistence. Many of us are taught to see a shift in goals as 'weakness' and 'failure'... If we 'fail' to achieve a goal, it's because there is something wrong with us. We didn't fight hard enough. We didn't 'believe.'"

Sometimes, of course, you get there. You make up your mind that you're going to give up. It could be a job you need to let go of, or a lover. If you're a grackle, it could be that seed on the bottom of the yellow cup. "This isn't working for me," you think, "and I'm exhausting myself for nothing." So you do what Alyn and Sneed did. Or what honeybees and crows do. You quit—so that you'll have the time and the energy to go after something else. Something more promising.

And it all begins with the twitch of a neuron.

PERMISSION SLIP

You want to quit. Deep inside, you just *know*: it's time. When a situation doesn't feel right, listen to your body and your mind. Giving up and going in another direction is a survival strategy, just as it is for other animals. Don't let the fear of being called a quitter keep you from protecting yourself from physical and mental harm.

_____

Chapter Two

The Neuroscience of "Nope—I'm Done"

I think intention and willpower...are highly
overrated. You rarely achieve anything with
those things.

—June Huh

Todd Parker knew the signs.

Just five years before, he'd given up a tenured teaching
position at DePaul University in Chicago. It was the perfect gig
for him, or so he'd thought. It was precisely the kind of job he'd
dreamed about while earning his doctorate in English literature at
Cornell University. But he quit DePaul in 2006 in order to become
a Franciscan monk. Parker was sent to serve in San Francisco, working in a soup kitchen.

Four years later, there it was again, that familiar feeling: the itch
to quit. The conviction that he was on the wrong path. The religious
life didn't satisfy his soul as he'd hoped it would. He no longer felt
a calling.

So he quit for the second time. Enrolled in nursing school. Returned
to New Mexico, where he'd been born and raised, and began working

at a facility that provides medical care to disabled adults. At last, he assures me when I call to ask how it's going, he's found his life.

"You can pose the narrative as heroic change," Parker says, "but to me, it was motivated more by fear. Fear of turning into something that was very short of what I'd envisioned for myself, professionally and ethically. Fear of becoming moribund."

Each time Parker quit—leaving the classroom and then the cloister—it was easy to track what happened on the *outside*. He moved from Chicago to San Francisco to Albuquerque. He went from tweed jacket to cassock to scrubs.

Yet what happened on the *inside*—within the spidery, cracked-mirror maze of his approximately eighty-six billion neurons, roughly the same amount each of us has—actually was more significant, because it marked the starting point. The first instant he considered quitting, this was it: the site where his quitting really began, as electrical pulses and chemicals zipped and fizzed among those brain cells, directing what he did and when he did it.

Informed by fascinating experiments undertaken in the past several years with zebrafish, mice, and rats, researchers now know more than ever before about the neuroscience of giving up: how a particular kind of cell, motivated by a special set of chemical triggers, "quits"—that is, ceases an action.

If you're a human being, that action might be resigning from a job. Or leaving a spouse. Or lighting up—or not—the next cigarette. The point is that everything we do—from small, trifling gestures made with a second's worth of reflection all the way up to large, momentous, life-changing actions that come after months or years of contemplation—involves quitting one path for another.

"For humans, there are many ways in which we abandon behaviors," Dr. Misha Ahrens tells me. "Some of those ways we might have in common with a fish."

In his lab at the Janelia Research Campus at the Howard Hughes Medical Institute in Ashburn, Virginia, Ahrens and his team routinely observe a phenomenon that, until recently, had never been glimpsed in real time: the entire brain of a living organism as it decides a task is futile and quits. Using techniques such as genetic engineering and three-dimensional microscopy, these neuroscientists are able to watch a fish brain in the process of giving up. The hope is that one day we will be able to apply that information to the complexity and sophistication of human brains.

The new science of quitting has great potential to improve our lives, Ahrens and his colleagues believe. The discoveries could help in the search for effective treatments for drug and alcohol addiction. Or bring relief from psychiatric afflictions such as obsessive-compulsive disorder and other self-destructive conditions. Or offer ways to enhance cognitive flexibility. Because quitting lies at the heart of human endeavor. It's about behavior and decision-making. It's about motivation and initiative. It's about choice and aspiration. It's about depression and anxiety—and recovery. It's about why we start and stop and start again.

And for Ahrens and his fellow neuroscientists, the quest begins in the brain of a creature that's smaller than a paint chip.

———————

We know everything and nothing about the brain.

"Even the basic operational principles governing a brain's interconnectedness of cells have remained painfully elusive," Dr. Florian Engert, a legendary professor of molecular and cellular biology at Harvard University, has written.

We know *how* someone drinks a cup of coffee, because it's easy to see: they grasp the mug handle with a couple of curved fingers and a thumb, they take a sip, they set the mug back down again. The action can be observed by anybody who cares to watch: the grip, the lift, the slurp. But understanding the complex interface between the coffee drinker's intention and their subsequent action—the part we *can't* see? The link, that is, between neuron and Nespresso?

Much, *much* more difficult.

Engert was Ahrens's supervisor at the Harvard lab before the latter established his own lab a decade ago. While working for Engert on a postdoctoral fellowship, Ahrens was part of a team that performed a revolutionary experiment, one that stunned the brain-science world: the imaging of a living organism's neurons—approximately one hundred thousand in this case, because it was a zebrafish—in action. Previously, only bits and pieces of neural activity had been observed at any one time.

"We tried to push the boundaries of what these animals can do," recalls Ahrens of his time in Engert's lab. "There are big differences in the brain from moment to moment."

An observation that Ahrens made during that historic, whole-body imaging experiment—the way a zebrafish would swim vigorously and then stop—"stayed in the back of my mind," he recalls to me. "I picked it up again when I started my own lab. This drastic switching of behavior was interesting. A brain is never static. But how can it suddenly do such a hugely different thing? Something's going on inside the brain."

The fish, he realized, were doing what all animals do, too, including humans: quitting and then resuming their activity, over and over again. But how? And in response to which signals in the brain?

———

Until the final decades of the twentieth century, scientists could only tell what the brain was up to by identifying and measuring the chemicals flashing between neurotransmitters. This enabled them to "look at what *fueled* neural activity, which is a bit like trying to understand a car's engine by studying gasoline," writes Bessel van der Kolk. Then came the game-changer: imaging technology able to capture the brain in action as it goes about its work. "Neuroimaging," he explains, "made it possible to see inside the engine."

For neuroscientists such as Ahrens and Michael Bruchas, a professor at the University of Washington whose studies are aimed at helping people with addiction issues, neuroimaging spotlights the mechanisms by which the brain functions, second by second, synapse by synapse.

Yet even when armed with the most sophisticated imaging devices ever devised, figuring out how the brain does what it does still is a daunting challenge for researchers. Not only are brains incredibly complex to begin with, but they never stand still. "Neurons—influenced by genes, the environment, and more recently by addictive drugs—change their shape and connectivity constantly," Bruchas tells me from his campus office in Seattle. "Multiple components change."

Science writer Ariel Sabar came up with a handy metaphor to describe the daisy-chain nature of the brain, its vast and intricate interconnectedness: "The cells exchange messages in the form of electrical pulses, which race at millisecond speeds along networks of fibers spanning every region of the brain," Sabar wrote in *Smithsonian Magazine*. "At almost every moment...the brain's Beijing is on the phone to its Helsinki, with La Paz and Kampala patched in on conference."

And that's true of the briefest, simplest, most ordinary and inane

activity in which the brain engages, such as grabbing that quick cup
of joe. So good luck trying to envision how it solves a crossword
puzzle or composes a symphony or performs a cartwheel or decides
whether or not to quit law school. A behavior like giving up—even
if it's just the temporary stopping of a tail swish by an animal as tiny
as a zebrafish—still is breathtakingly complex.

By the way, if you're wondering why neuroscience labs use zebrafish for their experiments, and why labs such as Ahrens's and Engert's
have long rows of shelves stacked up with identical containers in
which zebrafish swim, awaiting the summons to go to work, I wondered the same thing. It turns out those hardy tropical minnows,
typically found in freshwater streams in India and South Asia, are
cheap and easy to procure, and they reproduce quickly. They also
have genes with which scientists can easily tinker, manipulating
those genes so that the neurons flash bright green when busy. Moreover, zebrafish are transparent in the larval stage. Sabar puts it like
this: "To read the minds of baby zebrafish...all you had to do was
look."

———

Zebrafish instinctively swim against the current, making slow but
steady progress. To thwart that powerful drive and frustrate the
fish until they want to quit, Ahrens's team uses virtual reality. They
equip a tank with visual feedback: a screen upon which they project
moving bars. Those bars make the zebrafish believe they are making
no progress despite their efforts. To the fish, no matter how hard
they swim, they feel as if they are going nowhere fast.

The animals' first response, Ahrens tells me, is to try harder. They
expend increasing amounts of energy to try and propel themselves
forward. After a short period of time, though, they give up. They

enter a state he calls "futility-induced passivity." That should sound familiar; as we learned in chapter 1, animals can't use up too much valuable energy on a pointless task or they will perish.

Using imaging techniques, Ahrens and his team are able to trace what's happening inside the zebrafish brain when the moment of quitting occurs, pinpointing the specific neuron that is involved in prompting the animals' behavior. Identifying this neuron was a major step forward in the science of giving up. But during the early days of their research, the zebrafish threw them a curve.

Instead of a neuron, Ahrens recalls, what triggered first when the fish capitulated was another type of brain cell—found in humans as well as fish and all other animals—called a glial cell. Unlike neurons, glial cells don't make electrical impulses. Sometimes called helpers or housekeeping cells, glial cells were thought to only support the more significant neurons, rather like a pit crew for a flashy racing car. "Neurons are optimized to be super-fast," Ahrens tells me. "Glial cells were known to operate slower." Scientists now believe, however, that glial cells have a bigger role to play than previously understood and are crucial to essential functions such as memory processing and immune system response. Under a microscope, these glial cells look like scruffy starbursts, weaving their tentacles around the neurons whose operations they support.

"People have done imaging of glial cells. They knew there was activity in them—we just didn't know what it was for," Ahrens says. "I've always had trouble believing that they were only there to keep the neurons healthy."

Of the three kinds of glial cells, Ahrens adds, the ones known as radial astrocytes were activated at the moment the fish gave up.

According to a report on the experiment published in 2019 in *Cell* magazine, here's the brief rundown of what happens: glial cells track the zebrafish's efforts and, when a threshold is crossed—researchers don't yet know what it is, but might be a certain number of attempts—the message is sent. It's a blunt one: *quit.*

So it's the previously unsung astrocyte, not the much-heralded neuron, that reacts to the fish's frustration and enables the animal to throw in the towel.

"We established that astrocytes were essential in completing this neural circuit," Ahrens tells me. That was a big deal in the neuroscience world. "There has been a lot of hypothesizing about what astrocytes could do. But it had not been clarified in a living brain."

To double-check his hypothesis, Ahrens used a laser to disable the astrocytes involved in the process of quitting. The result was a fish that would delight a latter-day Vince Lombardi—a fish without an "off" switch. "If you remove or silence those [astrocyte] cells," Ahrens says, "you get a fish that basically never gives up."

And when Ahrens's team manipulated the astrocytes so that those glial cells remained active, they created the opposite: a fish that was all too willing to quit, that would readily stop swimming. The scientists didn't have to resort to the virtual reality trick of making the fish believe their efforts were pointless. With the astrocytes switched on, the fish didn't even bother trying to persevere.

———————

No disrespect intended to zebrafish, but what do these breakthroughs mean for human beings? What's the payoff for you and for me and for anybody who's trying to craft a happier and more productive life?

We know that quitting is a core function of the brain. These "basic science studies," as Ahrens refers to them, help lay the groundwork for the next level: applied science and medicine. In neuroscience, you can't skip steps. Insights build on one another. Might astrocytes be tweaked to regulate the impulse to quit—or not quit—in human brains?

"It could very well be," Ahrens muses, "that we enter the same kind of passive state as a result of the same mechanism. But it's unknown."

For now, the ultimate implications of his work for human beings may be many years and many experiments away. These days, Ahrens and his team continue to investigate how the astrocytes do what they do. Among the questions is this: Which chemicals are released in what order, suppressing or initiating the activity in the neurons, that tell the fish to quit or keep going?

All Ahrens can say for sure is that we're inching closer than ever before to understanding how the brain regulates effort—and halts that effort when it isn't contributing to the organism's survival prospects. And even though his own work requires unremitting effort over a long period of time, he takes my point about the dubious value of grit: "'Never give up'—I don't like that," he muses. "It's not always the right strategy. You need to ignore the fact that you've put in a lot of effort. It doesn't make the outcome any more valuable."

———

Michael Bruchas thinks a lot about thinking.

It's part of his job description as a neuroscientist. But in talking with him—and hearing his excitement when he describes the strides that he and his thirty-person lab at the University of Washington have made in recent years—you realize that it's a lot more than a nine-to-five thing with him. "I'm very passionate about this," Bruchas confirms.

His official title is proof of the sprawling complexity of his work. He's a professor of anesthesiology and pain medicine and pharmacology, with joint appointments in the department of bioengineering and in the college's Center of Excellence in Neurobiology of Addiction, Pain, and Emotion.

Bruchas knows the gifts and glories of the brain, how it enables us to climb mountains and knit scarves and write sonnets and solve mathematical equations and whip up a soufflé. But he's also aware of how that same organ can bring terrible suffering and sustained emotional pain to those afflicted with mental illnesses, from clinical depression to schizophrenia and anxiety disorders, from dependence on drugs and alcohol to excessive eating and obsessive-compulsive disorders.

The more we know about the brain, Bruchas believes, the closer we'll get to being able to relieve that suffering. And the more we know about quitting—the moments when the brain decides to change behavior—the more we'll know about the brain as a whole.

 WHITE FLAG MOMENT

I decided that I would understand Einstein's theory. I would find a book and translate all the unfamiliar words into ones I understood. So I went off to the Widener Library to look for a book, preferably one by Einstein, since he obviously understood the theory. The first three pages went fairly nicely. But on the second day, I ran into an equation [that was incomprehensible]. Thus ended my attempt. I had hit a wall. That was the important step...By the end of my sophomore year, I felt I understood enough of at least the philosophical background of relativity that a chat with Einstein might be helpful.

—*Jeremy Bernstein*

"There are two populations who would be helped" by his research on quitting, Bruchas explains. "Depressed people who are not motivated enough. And on the opposite side is the substance abuser, who is *very* motivated—but toward the wrong things. If we can target certain receptors, we can modulate certain behaviors. Our focus is on understanding neuro-modulation.

"In the brain," he continues, "you have electrical signals and you have chemical signals. We're focused on the chemical transmitters that are the modulators." In experiments with mice and rats, "we dial up and dial down the chemical signals." These signals, he tells me, are received by "a class of receptors that have evolved over thousands of years. We're trying to understand the messengers."

In 2019, Bruchas and his team reported a breakthrough: they pinpointed the place where the interaction occurs between the neurons involved with motivation—called nociceptin neurons—and the receptors with which they link up, and just how that interaction happens. In the part of the brain called the ventral tegmental area (VTA), these special neurons release nociceptin, which suppresses dopamine. The VTA is located in the center of the brain.

Most of us are familiar with dopamine these days because of its rep as the brain's party planner, making sure everyone's having a good time. It's responsible for the pleasurable feelings we get from things like food, sex, and music. But dopamine, essentially a chemical messenger that pings between neurons, is associated with motivation as well as good times. Squelch the dopamine—which is among the things that nociceptin molecules do—and you've got a quitter on your hands.

In their experiments, Bruchas and his colleagues noticed that, at just about the same moment a mouse decides they've had enough and stops doing what they're doing, the nociceptin neurons become more active. Dopamine is suppressed by the release of the nociceptin, which, Bruchas explains, sends out a protein that binds to the receptors and blocks the dopamine uptake. Without the sense of satisfaction supplied by the dopamine, the mouse gets discouraged and quits.

So do the nociceptin neurons trigger the quitting—or does the quitting trigger the nociceptin neurons?

"We don't know yet," Bruchas acknowledges. The answer—which he and his team are working assiduously to determine—could add details to the bigger picture that one day may offer relief to people struggling with problems like compulsive gambling and other addictions.

"You can imagine a person at a slot machine," he tells me. "They put in their money over and over again. They'll just keep doing it. But at some point, there's a threshold. They give up." He and his colleagues replicated that scenario in the lab: If a mouse poked a button with their nose, they received a pellet of food. " 'You want another? Now you have to poke two times. Now four. Now sixteen.' It works on an exponential scale. Eventually the mouse says, 'I'm not going to do it one hundred times.' They reach their breaking point."

We all know the feeling: a moment comes when we've simply had enough. We snap. We may call it "the last straw" or "the straw that broke the camel's back." We're fed up. So we stop.

Observing the animal's brain at that instant—call it the "Nope—I'm done" moment—and seeing how it coincides with the sudden ramping up of the nociceptin neurons was a crucial discovery, Bruchas says. His hope is that the R & D division of some pharmaceutical company will one day create drugs to manipulate the activity in the VTA, helping to break the grip of addiction.

"But it's tricky," he cautions. "We don't know what's happening in other cells. You might want to block one thing but not something else. We're always asking ourselves, 'Why is that part of the brain there? Why was it designed that way?' Perseverance is regulated naturally by the brain, possibly through multiple pathways."

———————

For our brains, quitting is not simple. In fact, it's among the most difficult maneuvers we ever ask them to do, says Dr. Thilo Womelsdorf of Vanderbilt University, because it requires a capacity that researchers are only beginning to understand in its full breadth and complexity: cognitive flexibility.

But the good news is that the more times you ask your brain to do something it's never done before, to try something new—that is, to go in another direction after it has quit the present one—the better it gets at doing that. An active brain is a happy brain. Quitting is like aerobics for your brain.

In recent experiments, Womelsdorf tells me, researchers have discovered how challenging it is for the brain to make what he calls "stay or go" decisions: "In order for the brain to know if it should change or switch to doing something new, it must integrate all the other options that are available. What else is out there? How much have you already received and how much will you get? To have the material you need to decide if you should stay or go, many areas of the brain must be connected."

Womelsdorf, an associate professor of psychology and computer science at Vanderbilt, explains from his office in Nashville that our brains appear to have special areas reserved for just this purpose: exercising the flexibility to change course—or *not* to change course, if the current situation is deemed to be better than what it will find after the change.

In a 2020 report published in *Proceedings of the National Academy of Science*, Womelsdorf and his colleagues in the university's departments of engineering and informatics and at the Vanderbilt Brain Institute discussed the results of experiments showing where those areas are located and how they function.

"There are several brain areas that we know are responsible," Womelsdorf says. One promising area is found below the outer cortical mantle in the basal ganglia, which is home to neurons that enable us to master the fine motor skills required for activities like playing the piano. Womelsdorf and his colleagues speculate that the same physical flexibility that allows, say, a hand to stretch an octave on a piano keyboard also helps the brain in its decisional flexibility as it mulls over options and strategies and potential outcomes.

In conjunction with the Centre for Vision Research at York University in Toronto, Womelsdorf and his fellow researchers performed experiments in which they measured brain cell activity during the performance of tricky tasks such as making choices from an array of possibilities. The brain responded with gusto, becoming more active when a problem proved especially daunting.

Once a challenge was mastered—once the brain became certain of the outcome—neuronal activity diminished. Yet a fresh problem caused it to ratchet right back up again. In the brain, familiarity breeds complacency.

Kianoush Banaie Boroujeni, a researcher on Womelsdorf's team who served as first author on the report, put it this way in a summary of the findings: "These neurons seem to help the brain circuits to reconfigure and transition from formerly relevant information and a tenuous connection to attend to new, relevant information." The brain, in other words, gets a real kick out of rising to the challenge.

The brain's plasticity—its ability to change throughout our lives and to adapt to new circumstances, in effect rewiring itself when it needs to—now is well-known. Scientists used to think that the brain was basically a black box: the number of neurons you had at birth were all you'd ever have. But we know better now. Plasticity is how people in their seventies learn how to play the bassoon or to dance the tango. It's how Todd Parker was able to go from being a

literature professor to a registered nurse, mastering an entirely different skill set as well as a great deal of new information.

But what if the brain's not able to do those things? Sometimes, an
incapacity either innate or acquired can interfere with cognition. If
the neurons that enable cognitive flexibility aren't functioning properly, Womelsdorf says, people may not be *able* to switch their attention from one task to another. They're stuck. They can't adapt to a
new environment. Conversely, their attention might switch *too* easily, and they have the opposite problem: they're "unable to concen-
trate on important information for any length of time." Womelsdorf
hopes that his research may one day help people who suffer from
obsessive-compulsive disorder and similar issues. Toward that end,
he and his colleagues in other departments at Vanderbilt are developing drugs to treat illnesses such as schizophrenia, and diseases
that cause mental decline such as Alzheimer's. Knowing more about
what happens in the brain as it goes about its work, and where and
how that work occurs, will help in that effort, he says.

Yet with all that we know, we are barely at the threshold of fully
understanding the neural networks that underlie cognitive flexibility,
Womelsdorf cautions. Neurons engage in "very fast switching and
changing" that enables us to make decisions to give up or keep going.
"There are neurons in the brain that inhibit other neurons when you
need to quit a behavior. It disinhibits the stuff you want to do. These
neuronal events enable us to quit one thing and do another."

Indeed, there may be "circuits that cause you to quit and try
something else." His research has an overall goal that's simultaneously finger-snap simple and astonishingly complex: "Find them."

———————

Brains thrive on challenges. As researchers have demonstrated in
a variety of experiments, quitting one activity and commencing

another captivates the brain, beefing up its problem-solving capacity and sharpening its performance as it undertakes new tasks. In that way, we're a lot like other animals: our brains, when functioning properly, seem designed to quit regularly and strategically.

In one crucial way, however, we don't resemble those other creatures at all—and that distinction hints at a possible cause of our conflicted attitude toward quitting. Even when quitting is the smart choice, something may interfere with our making it.

"Some of the time we are indeed just like any other animal," writes Sapolsky in *Behave: The Biology of Humans at Our Best and Worst*, and researchers can lump us in with other creatures and make broad generalizations about what we do and why. But not always, he adds: "Sometimes the only way to understand our humanness is to consider solely humans, because the things we do are unique...We construct cultures premised on beliefs concerning the nature of life and can transmit those beliefs multi-generationally."

No matter how much we may like to believe that we're independent thinkers, and that we make our own decisions, we're part of the larger social world. We can't escape it. Our brains aren't hermetically sealed engines of pure thought. As van der Kolk reminds us, "The social environment interacts with brain chemistry." And naturalist Bernd Heinrich puts it this way in his book *Life Everlasting: The Animal Way of Death*: "Culture is like the chalk and limestone made from the organisms of past ages under our feet. It's the residue of our knowledge, foibles, and aspirations that have accumulated over the ages. It's the nonmaterial life that we absorb into our brains through our eyes and ears, the way plants absorb nutrients through their roots."

We live in the midst of artistic representations of ideas—the novels, movies, TV series, songs, tweets, memes, ads, poems, billboards, slogans, Instagram posts, and video games that surround us. They shape us, creating our desires, influencing our attitudes and our actions.

They do something else for us, too: they tell us how to feel about quitting.

PERMISSION SLIP

You want to keep your brain nimble and flexible. But how? Brains are like bodies: they crave motion and change. So it's worthwhile to constantly reassess methods and goals. To reflect on alternative possibilities for your life. If you decide to give up, don't think of it as a surrender: think of it as aerobics for your brain.

Chapter Three

Jennifer Aniston Quits Her Job: The Fine Art of Saying, "So Long"

> It will be a little messy, but embrace the
> mess. It will be complicated, but rejoice in the
> complications...And don't be frightened. You can
> always change your mind. I know: I've had four
> careers and three husbands.
>
> —*Nora Ephron*

In a scene from the 1999 cult classic film *Office Space*, Joanna (Jennifer Aniston) is fed up with Stan—her bespectacled buffoon of a boss—and the silly buttons he makes her wear on her waitress uniform. When Stan tells her for the umpteenth time that she lacks "flair," she explodes.

Because she's done. Finished. She's had it up to *here*, got it?

What happens next has been viewed more than a million times on YouTube, a meme that signifies defiance against every stupid rule laid down by every moronic boss in every soul-sucking workplace since the beginning of time: Joanna declares, "I hate this job. I hate this goddamned job and I don't need it!"

With the flourish of a middle finger, she's gone.

The scene's popularity reveals just how deeply the act of quitting resonates. Because quitting may be born in our brains, but our brains live in the world—the cultural world, the world of *Office Space* and other creative illustrations of giving up.

No matter how we regard Joanna's gesture—as a principled blow for workers' rights in the struggle against the heartless corporate machine or as a petty snit fit—nobody's unmoved by it. Nobody's neutral. Similarly, nobody can watch with indifference the penultimate episode of the second season of HBO Max's 2022 hit series *Hacks*, when Jimmy (Paul W. Downs) dramatically quits his job at the management agency. You either cheer or squirm. You applaud—or you roll your eyes at his shortsighted foolishness. There's no middle ground. Which is why such scenes are a nifty index to gauge how you really feel about quitting.

After watching Jimmy and Joanna take their stand—might you be more inclined to do the same the next time a supervisor ticks you off? Or the opposite: If you're usually too rash, too madcap, will watching somebody else quit on impulse make you a little more patient and restrained? Maybe, in fact, that's what movies are actually *for*, muses Matthew Specktor in his memoir about Los Angeles, *Always Crashing in the Same Car*: to remind us of who we really are. "Art invites identification," he writes, adding, "I believe art and life chase each other." It's not that entertainment has to be didactic—only that we can quit vicariously through characters in movies and TV shows and novels before we take the leap ourselves, keeping an eye out for how that kind of renunciation makes us feel: smugly liberated or cringing and regretful.

"There's a reason these scenes become popular memes," says Emily Zemler, a London-based entertainment writer. "A single frame holds so much meaning." She cites the moment in *Mad Men* when Peggy

Olson (Elisabeth Moss) quits and "walks down the hallway with her box of stuff and a cigarette." We're drawn to these scenes because, Zemler tells me, "they become ciphers for our desires, especially ones we may not have the opportunity to act out ourselves. Quitting takes a lot of guts and it's a very risky move. Who hasn't wanted to tell off an annoying boss or depart a shitty job with memorable flair? It's a shared dream that very few of us actually get to fulfill."

But by and large, scenes like that aren't the cultural norm—which might be why they give us a subversive little thrill. More often, quitting has been depicted over the years as just about the worst thing you can do, as the last refuge of the lazy fraidy-cat. Our classic movie heroes are the guys and gals who don't give up: Will Kane, Gary Cooper's character in *High Noon* (1952), who faces the bad guys alone when the rest of the town turns yellow, or Rooster Cogburn (John Wayne) in *True Grit* (1969), who won't abandon his quest for justice, or Karen Silkwood (Meryl Streep) in *Silkwood* (1983), determined to expose the truth even when her life's at stake. Those iconic films have helped to reinforce the idea that quitting is the coward's way out.

"I think most people underestimate just how deeply we are impacted by the media around us," says Devon Price, social psychologist and author of *Laziness Does Not Exist: A Defense of the Exhausted, Exploited, and Overworked.* "So it is no surprise that being inundated with images of tough, gritty, independent heroes over and over again for decades has an intense impact on us.

"We are surrounded by media tropes from a very young age, and we are not taught to interrogate or question those messages," Price continues. "From the time we are very young, we are absolutely barraged with television programs, advertisements, films, and now, social media videos that we use to draw logical inferences about how the world works, who we are in that world, and how we are expected to behave. This impacts human behavior in many widely documented ways."

Cultural images are subtle but highly effective influences, Price believes. "We tend to passively consume media when we are tired, lonely, looking for an escape, and otherwise not in the frame of mind to question what we are taking in. This makes it very easy for our expectations and views to be molded by the media over time."

And that's precisely how, Price tells me, the myth of perseverance is able to do its dirty work before we're fully aware of it. "These mythologies of grit and perseverance are also deeply tied to our national myths about what America is, and to the Protestant work ethic and our religious and cultural programming. It only serves to deepen that conditioning."

No wonder most of us want to do a little dance when Joanna gives the finger to her clueless dweeb of a manager. Or when Jimmy rejects a direct order from his boss to dump Deborah Vance (Jean Smart) as a client because she's not young and hip—and quits instead. It's like watching the Charge of the Light Brigade.

Culture seeps into every corner of our lives. When Ezra Klein needed a title for his June 18, 2021, *New York Times* podcast about the economy in the wake of the pandemic, he didn't opt for one that referenced the Federal Reserve or mortgage-backed securities. He called it the "Welcome to the 'Take This Job and Shove It' Economy," referencing the famous 1978 country ballad written by David Allan Coe and sung by Johnny Paycheck.

Classic literature also is suffused with quitting themes, and no matter how long ago they were written, novels and plays bristle with moments of high drama that probably echo a dilemma you're facing right here, right now: Like Isabel Archer in Henry James's *The Portrait of a Lady* or Nora in Henrik Ibsen's *A Doll's House*, you might be dealing with a choice between quitting a so-so relationship and breaking free—or following convention and staying put. Like Ahab in *Moby-Dick*, you might be wrestling with an unhealthy obsession that you're desperate to relinquish.

And if you think all quitting scenes are mostly alike—somebody tosses out an ultimatum (or a harpoon) and storms away—and the emotions sparked by these scenes are all basically the same, you need to look deeper.

Quitting is *never* that simple.

———————

In the iconic 1982 film *An Officer and a Gentleman*, Mayo (Richard Gere) aspires to be a navy pilot. Yet he's managed to irritate Sergeant Foley (Louis Gossett Jr.) one too many times, and now Foley is trying to goad Mayo into dropping out by forcing him through a regimen of grueling physical feats. Pushed to the brink by pain and exhaustion, Mayo finally yells, "No sir! You can kick me outta here but I ain't quittin'!"

Here, the possibility of someone giving up kindles the opposite emotion from what we feel when Aniston's character bolts. In *Office Space*, quitting means freedom. In *An Officer and a Gentleman*, it means emotional devastation: Mayo's on the cusp of losing his comrades, his sense of belonging, his very identity. We're rooting for Joanna to bail on her job and walk out; if Mayo does that, however, we'll be crushed and heartbroken. Such moments tell us a great deal about ourselves—and our ambivalence about quitting, our love-hate relationship with succumbing to pressure and pulling out.

Maybe you're fond of the scene when Bridget Jones (Renée Zellweger) in *Bridget Jones's Diary* (2001) offers a great kiss-off line to her persnickety boss, Hugh Grant, before leaving the premises: "If staying here means working within ten yards of you, frankly I'd rather have a job wiping Saddam Hussein's ass." Or the excruciating but hilarious moment in *Jerry Maguire* (1996) when the title character played by Tom Cruise quits with panache, exhorting his colleagues to follow him out the door. Only Dorothy (Zellweger) does. Or the 2022 sitcom *Pivoting*, when a group of friends reacts to their friend's death by blowing up their tidy suburban lives and lurching toward the unknown. The most momentous break with convention: Sarah (Maggie Q) gives up her job as a trauma surgeon to work for minimum wage in a grocery store. And for the first time in her life, she's happy. (You may find that a tad too fantastical, but a friend of mine is an ER doc and she tells me it's her favorite moment in any TV show ever, and a career move she dreams of emulating—especially after a week of overnight shifts.)

Far more often, though, quitting is shown in a negative light. In the opening moments of the 2021 premiere of the sitcom *Abbott Elementary*, an anonymous teacher marches out the front door of the school, clutching a small cardboard box crammed with her belongings: rulers, pencils, coffee mug. Without looking back, she flips the bird to the ragtag inner-city school. (Unlike Aniston's parting shot, this one's pixilated.) She's giving up on the kids because they're too much for her. This kind of quitting isn't noble. It's shabby and selfish.

Watching these scenes can be therapeutic, Zemler theorizes: "When a character we love quits, we get to feel their tenacity and boldness for ourselves. That feeling can inspire viewers to make big moves themselves, or offer a sense of encouragement that we're not alone in wanting to leave dead-end, meaningless jobs." Or the meaningful ones, too, that have become too stressful.

———————

Many quitting scenes start out funny, with an over-the-top flurry of renunciation like Aniston's crude farewell in *Office Space*, but after a while the chuckle dies in your throat and you get a sense that something more serious is going on, and that everything henceforth is uncharted and maybe even a little unhinged. A crackle of apprehension runs through these movies, a frisson of recklessness and fear. Whatever is being left behind, be it a job or a kid or a husband or wife or any kind of adult responsibility, is like the last bit of solid ground before a free fall into nobody knows what. Anarchy's fun—but only temporarily.

 WHITE FLAG MOMENT

The character I played [in *The Colbys*] was Constance Colby Patterson...I quit the show after the first season. I seemed to be saying the same things week after week—the only way people could see any difference in performance was the fact that I had a different dress on...Constance wasn't going anyplace—but I was—I quit!

—*Barbara Stanwyck*

And sometimes, the quitting moment can seem zany and cool as it happens, but later a sobering reality sets in. The audience—like the characters who have chucked it all in an impulsive moment—wonders, "What now?" That's what happens in the famous final scene of *The Graduate* (1967), when Elaine (Katharine Ross) abruptly leaves her fiancé at the altar in order to run off with Benjamin (Dustin Hoffman). Sitting side by side on the getaway bus, their expressions wilt, going from excitement to dubious uncertainty. *What the hell have we done?* their faces seem to say. Quitting always carries a price.

Tammy (2014) follows a troubled, recently fired woman (Melissa McCarthy) as she tells the world to go screw itself and hits the road with her feisty grandmother (Susan Sarandon). It begins as one of those oh-no-she-didn't romps, but gradually a kind of creeping dread takes over as you watch: one thing after another goes awry. Nothing is safe or predictable, and it's weird and unsettling. *Eddie and the Cruisers* (1983) tells the story of a rock star (Michael Paré) who disappears just as his career is getting traction, and the mystery about why he quits is never resolved. The quitting in these films isn't refreshing and funny. It's desperate and edgy and dangerous.

Quitting pops up repeatedly in our favorite stories, a testament to its central place in the experience of being human. When we find ourselves laughing at it in a sitcom or singing along with it in a lyric or being deeply moved by it in a drama, we're reminded that the act of giving up is momentous and transformative. Reading a poem like "Do Not Go Gentle into That Good Night" by Dylan Thomas, in which a dying father is urged to resist death, to "rage against the dying of the light," can leave us shaken—but in one of two very different ways.

Some people find the poem incredibly compelling, interpreting it as a powerful testament to the importance of battling for life down to the very last breath, as an urgent brief for never giving up. Others see it as an unwillingness to accept the inevitability of death. What is it for you? The issue of quitting—in this case, quitting life itself—is a sort of Rorschach test for our attitudes about a journey that we all must take eventually.

———

"And saying yes to this version of her life would mean saying no to another version of her life," muses the narrator in Dana Spiotta's 2021 novel, *Wayward*, which has a simple but cataclysmic act of quitting at its core. "Whatever she was—the sum total of fifty-three years on this earth in this body—was insufficient to what would come next. She clearly had to change."

The "she" in the novel is Samantha Raymond, an upper-middle-class woman who's having trouble sleeping. She's having trouble with a lot of things, actually, from marriage to motherhood. Her husband doesn't get her. Her teenage daughter ignores her. Sam's own mother is dying. She's at loose ends. And so what does she do? She buys an old house and moves into it. By herself.

Sam gives up on her life as it is in order to get...what? That's the risk: sometimes you don't know until you do it, and by then it's too late to *un*do it.

"Quitting is a negative word," says Spiotta from her office at Syracuse University, where she teaches creative writing. "But you have to quit before you can do something else. The house speaks to her. She lets herself be seduced by the possibility of another life. Maybe she can remake herself by moving to another place."

  WHITE FLAG MOMENT

I quit college in my sophomore year. I thought that's what I needed to do to become a writer. That was pretty dramatic. And I've been divorced. You can get so invested in the status quo. Inertia settles in. You don't realize how stuck you were until you're out of it. It takes a leap to quit.

—*Dana Spiotta*

By writing *Wayward*, the author tells me, she was trying to "grapple with the question—'Can you really leave your past behind?' Maybe you can't. You can start over, try to be happy. But you feel society's judgment, if you quit a job or a marriage."

Quitting works well as a plot device because it's "dramatic and complicated," Spiotta says. "It's hard to know if you're doing something because you're running away from something or running toward it."

Spiotta's novel is in good company. Reinvention through a bold act of quitting is a seminal act for characters in classic literature, from Huck Finn and Jim heading down the river in Mark Twain's *Adventures of Huckleberry Finn* (1884) to Jay Gatsby's escape from his past in F. Scott Fitzgerald's *The Great Gatsby* (1925).

Your reaction to such novels—do the actions of the main characters make you think, "I get it!" or "WTF?"—may tell you how much control you believe any individual ultimately has over their life. Can you quit your family and recreate yourself from scratch, as Gatsby does? Can you change your life by quitting civilization and heading down the river on a raft? Or will you just end up circling back around to who you were in the first place?

As Adam Phillips writes in his 2022 essay "On Giving Up" in the *London Review of Books*, quitting energizes the stories of Franz Kafka and the plays of Shakespeare, especially *Macbeth* and *King Lear*, and the essays of Sigmund Freud. "Our history of giving up— that is to say, our attitude towards it, our obsession with it, our disavowal of its significance—may be a clue to...the beliefs, the sentences, around which we have organized ourselves," writes Phillips, a psychotherapist.

He comes up with an inventive definition of tragic heroes: They are "catastrophic examples of the inability to give up." It's a new way to look at Lear, Hamlet, Macbeth, and Othello, characters driven by compulsions of which they can't rid themselves such as revenge, ambition, and jealousy, states of mind that hold them captive more definitively than a bad guy with a gun.

The tension between quitting or not is what makes the topic so ideal for drama, Phillips writes: "We tend to think of giving up, in the ordinary way, as a lack of courage. We tend to value, and even idealize, the idea of seeing things through, of finishing things rather than abandoning them. Giving up has to be justified in a way that completion does not; giving up doesn't usually make us proud of ourselves; it is a falling short of our preferred selves."

Yet for Captain Ahab, the character in furious search of the titular white whale in Herman Melville's *Moby-Dick*, quitting is the opposite. It's the one thing he wants to master but can't; it's the goal he can't achieve. Not being able to quit his long quest is the cause of his torment: "What is it, this nameless, inscrutable, unearthly thing is it; what cozening, hidden lord and master, and cruel, remorseless emperor commands me; that against all natural lovings and longings I so keep pushing; and crowding, and jamming myself on all the time..." he roars and moans to Starbuck in the classic novel first published in 1851.

"Take This Job and Shove It" is a long way from Mozart's *Don Giovanni*, but both set the idea of quitting to music. In the latter, Donna Elvira begs the title character to abandon his philandering ways. No dice. Realizing that it's never going to happen, she throws up her hands. Don Giovanni pays a heavy price for his lascivious conduct—if, that is, you think being dragged off to hell is a less-than-ideal way to spend your golden years—and Donna Elvira heads for the convent.

That summary comes from Roger Pines, dramaturg at Lyric Opera of Chicago for almost a quarter of a century. When I asked him about quitting themes in well-known operas, he didn't hesitate; he came up with a long list faster than you can finish your drink at intermission once the lights have dimmed. A few highlights:

In Verdi's *La Traviata*, Violetta gives up her hope of bliss with Alfredo, having first renounced her life as a courtesan. In Jacques

Offenbach's *La Perichole*, Perichole quits her life on the streets with Piquillo; and in Richard Wagner's *Das Rheingold*, Alberich is forced to relinquish the ring he created. "Alberich curses the ring and then all the trouble begins," Pines explains, which "lasts over the course of three more operas." Quitting—be it love or happiness or life itself—is at the very heart of opera, he tells me.

  WHITE FLAG MOMENT

When I was eighteen, I just thought, "I'm not going to play this anymore." The clarinet was my passion. Something I really loved. I remember thinking, "I'm really good at this!" But I thought I had to have a career where I'd make money. And I was a terrible quitter as a kid—because I was a perfectionist...I picked up a clarinet last weekend. First time in forty years! All the musical knowledge came back.

—Diane Casey

The shadow of quitting falls across every page of *Bartleby, the Scrivener*, Melville's mesmerizing 1853 novella. Here the depiction of giving up is the opposite of what's found in *Moby-Dick*. Ahab wants to quit but can't; Bartleby's quitting accelerates, until finally he does nothing *but* quit. Neither fate is what you'd call optimal.

Bartleby, a man of "quiet mysteries," has a job copying documents in a Wall Street office. At first his work is acceptable, although he refuses some tasks with a deadpan "I would prefer not to." Gradually this escalates into an unwillingness to do anything. "At last, in reply to my urgings," recalls the narrator, "he informed me that he had permanently given up copying." Finally, he must be forcibly removed from the office.

Bartleby dies in jail, "huddled at the base of a wall, his knees drawn up, and lying on his side, his head touching the cold stones." His way of life—quitting—at last becomes his way of death.

If you don't relate to Bartleby and his habit of continuous quitting—and I hope for the sake of your own happiness that you find another role model—you might be drawn to the narrator in John Updike's short story "A&P," who quits in a beautifully useless gesture. First published in the *New Yorker* in 1961, the bittersweet tale has been anthologized constantly ever since, still more proof of the ongoing appeal of the drama of quitting.

"A&P" is narrated by a kid who works in a small grocery store. One summer afternoon, several young girls in bathing suits drift in. The crusty old manager is offended by the informality of their attire and tells them so, whereupon the kid, in a spontaneous act of gallantry, quits in protest: "I pull the bow at the back of my apron," he recounts, "and start shrugging it off my shoulders." At story's end, he doesn't have a job anymore and he knows he'll never see the girls again. "My stomach kind of fell," he muses mournfully, "as I felt how hard the world was going to be to me hereafter."

Culture matters, the biologist Heinrich reminds us: "We are not just the product of our genes. We are also the product of ideas...Ideas have long-lasting effects on us."

And those effects aren't always positive, especially when it comes to images of perseverance. Price offers this caution: "Much like the Horatio Alger novels of the past, today's popular media still teaches us to worship hard work and look down on the lazy."

Even worse is when Instagram influencers and YouTube celebrities claim that if only you don't quit, then you, too, can be rich and famous just like they are: "When massively successful stars attribute their good fortune entirely to how diligently they've worked," Price writes, "they set people up to have unrealistic expectations about the odds of success, and how wealth is actually meted out in this country."

As we bask in the blue glow of our screens, absorbing cultural messages about the perils of quitting and the splendors of grit, our brains are working away, assimilating those images and ideas. Yet if it feels like we arrived in the middle of the plot, it's because we did. Like any good superhero movie, perseverance has an origin story. A beginning. The idea that hanging in there at all costs is good—and giving up is always wrong—was *created*. Developed and nurtured for a specific purpose. Deliberately turned into idealized myth.

But where and by whom—and why?

PERMISSION SLIP

You've watched *Runaway Bride* a dozen times. You do a fist pump when Renée Zellweger tells off Hugh Grant in *Bridget Jones's Diary*. Quitting scenes make you feel bold and feisty, ready to make changes in your life. Or maybe not: perhaps they leave you nervous and apprehensive. Revisit your favorite quitting scenes. Your reaction may tell you a lot about your comfort level with change.

PART II

HOW "QUITTING" BECAME A DIRTY WORD—AND WHY IT MATTERS

Holding up hard work as the key to success allows us to maintain our belief in a just world and rationalize inequality.

—*Adam Grant*

Chapter Four

Peddling Perseverance

You know the saying "A winner never quits and a quitter never wins"? To which *Freakonomics Radio* says, "Are you sure? Sometimes quitting is strategic, and sometimes it can be your best possible plan."

—*Stephen J. Dubner*

When Heather Stone speaks, you can sometimes hear the faint rub of her native Kentucky, a gentle Southern lilt that's like a soft breeze tousling certain syllables. Mostly, though, her voice is pure Chicago: it has the flat, why-beat-around-the-bush flintiness of a woman who's been through a lot and doesn't mind sharing the details.

"It was definitely a very dark time," she tells me. "I took the leap blindly, thinking it would all work out. Well, it did—but not in the way I thought. I felt like a real failure. But I wasn't going to look back. I'd made my decision. I just had to deal with it."

Stone is a former colleague, and I'm catching up with her on a Sunday summer afternoon. She's just moved into her new house in central Florida with her partner, Kai, after a couple of decades spent braving the winters along Lake Michigan. It's a big change, she admits: "I look out the window and see Spanish moss and palm trees. Not a tall building in sight."

While she makes a grilled cheese sandwich, she tells me about the odyssey that took her from a job she loved—staff photographer at the *Chicago Tribune*, flying around the world to track the news in places like Ethiopia, Egypt, Japan, Poland, and France—to...whatever comes next. All she knows for sure is that it won't be photography.

"In hindsight," she says, "it all sort of needed to happen. But it was a tough time."

In 2008, after a dozen years at the *Tribune*, Stone quit her job to open a photography business in Chicago. "I quit on a high," she recalls. "Life was rosy. I took a leap of faith." But she didn't leap far: same city, same profession. To her family, though, the move was way too risky. "They were like, '*What?* You had a perfectly good job! And you *left!*'"

Business was only so-so. And she had a large mortgage on her house. The numbers just weren't working. Stone was getting nervous. So was the bank.

She returned to the *Tribune*—not as a staff photographer but as a technician in the photo lab for half of her old salary. And no trips to France or Egypt. "It was an exercise in humility," she admits. But she got a handle on her finances, which meant she was able to quit again. At that point she and Kai—he's also a photographer—looked at each other and realized they were both thinking the same thing: it was time to go.

Florida sounded interesting, especially after all those gray, gruesome winters in the Midwest. "It was the right time to make another transition and so I did it," Stone declares. "I'd lived in Chicago for twenty years and experienced it fully. It was time for something else."

They planned to rent at first but found the perfect house to buy.

Kai has steady work making wedding videos. Stone isn't sure what her next job will be—only that it won't involve cameras.

"I'm going to have to reinvent myself down here. I can go back to school, maybe. Just jump into something." She laughs. "I'm making up this shit as I go along. Just reacting to the universe."

Stone's personal odyssey wouldn't please Samuel Smiles. If, courtesy of a rip in the space-time continuum, you were able to go back to mid-Victorian London and tell him her story, he would shake his head. He would frown. He would murmur, *No, no, no.* He might even become so agitated and aghast that he'd sweat right through his double-breasted frock coat, the kind favored by gentlemen of that era: *Quitting your job? THRICE? Going in a wholly new direction? And the notion of "just reacting to the universe"—what species of madness is that?*

In 1859 Smiles published a book called *Self-Help: With Illustrations of Character and Conduct.* Stone's decision to change careers in midstream is precisely the opposite of what he preached ardently therein. Packed with inspirational biographies of successful men, from engineers to potters to geologists to sea captains, and bolstered with uplifting parables and rousing pep talks, *Self-Help* promoted the notion that perseverance is the quality without which one cannot hope to lead a happy and prosperous life. The book was a sensation—eagerly snapped up by readers and hotly discussed in taverns and constantly quoted in drawing rooms.

To understand how we got here—how, that is, in the twenty-first century quitting has become synonymous with failure, and why the phrase "giving up" makes most of us cringe with shame—we have to go back to roughly the midpoint of the nineteenth, when Smiles first began peddling perseverance the way traveling salesmen were touting magical elixirs to cure gout and heart palpitations.

Smiles, a Scot born in 1812, believed that you must pick a path and stick with it. You must not pivot. You must sneer at setbacks. You must smash through impediments. You must work hard and—this is crucial—never, *never* quit.

"He invented the self-help market at just the right time," Peter Sinnema tells me. An English professor at the University of Alberta, Sinnema wrote the introduction to the Oxford World's Classics edition of *Self-Help* and is, therefore, an expert on the history of grit. He knows all about the cultural conditions in nineteenth-century Britain, a time when the Industrial Revolution was changing everything, when vast fortunes were being made by a few—while life for most people was an ordeal of relentless poverty. The more thoughtful and sensitive members of the reading public needed a way to reconcile this vast disparity in fortunes. And it was Smiles's particular genius, Sinnema says, to recognize that readers didn't want drab moral lessons—they much preferred colorful stories about successful people, with details about how they got ahead by toughing it out.

"Smiles created a niche market within a field of human desire that knew what it wanted," Sinnema says. "He created something new—he made the biography into an inspirational form. In an emerging market economy, it was important to push oneself ahead in that ruthless world. It was, 'If someone else can do it, I can do it, too.' The idea was that if you were energetic enough, you could be successful."

Which means, of course, that the reverse was also true: If you *weren't* successful, that surely meant you didn't try hard enough. You had dithered. You had drifted. You were fickle and feckless. Worst of all, you gave up.

The same year *Self-Help* appeared, Charles Darwin finally published his *On the Origin of Species by Means of Natural Selection*. "This was a rich moment in perceiving humanity's place in the world," Sinnema says.

What Darwin's ideas did in reference to the natural world—blasting through old certainties with tornadic force—Smiles's did to the cultural one. His book insisted that only hard work and perseverance could give you a worthwhile life. Nuances such as dumb luck and fortunate birth? Banished. And for the next forty years, Smiles published sequels with titles like *Character* (1871) and *Thrift* (1875). These books, equally popular, pounded the point home: it's up to you to make your way in the world. If you falter, it's on you. Nobody else. And it's certainly not the fault of government policies or the courts: "No laws, however stringent," Smiles wrote scoldingly in *Self-Help*, "can make the idle industrious, the thriftless provident, or the drunken sober. Such reforms can only be effected by means of individual action, economy, and self-denial; by better habits, rather than by greater rights."

The stories in *Self-Help* all make the same point: your destiny rests in your own hands. If you're not rich, if you're not powerful, if you're not fulfilled, it's because you didn't do what the people in Smiles's book did: you didn't dig deep and sweat and sacrifice. Your lot in life is your own doing. Don't bother blaming anyone else.

Benjamin Franklin is often tagged with the sobriquet "patron saint of the self-help movement," as Walter Isaacson dubs him in *Benjamin Franklin: An American Life*. It's true that *Poor Richard's Almanack* came first: Franklin initially published it in 1732, more than a century before *Self-Help* appeared. *Poor Richard* "helped launch a craze that persists to this day, for books featuring simple rules and secrets about how to succeed in business and in life,"

Isaacson writes. Franklin's work—which, like *Self-Help*, sold fabulously well—contained "genial moral maxims," his biographer notes, along with filler such as recipes, trivia, and gossip.

Self-Help, though, is a different thing altogether. It's a systematic and highly detailed blueprint of how to prosper and conquer, not simply a cheerful list of life hacks. It's not just homilies and folksy aphorisms. Nor is it amusing, as *Poor Richard* often is. Its purpose is not to entertain, but to prod, to motivate, through sharing the stories of "distinguished inventors, artists, thinkers, and workers of all kinds," as Smiles wrote, all of whom "owe their success, in a great measure, to an indefatigable industry and application."

Smiles's big idea surged through the late nineteenth and twentieth centuries: the difference between rich and poor is exclusively the fault of the latter. The gap surely couldn't be attributed to the greed and corruption and lack of social conscience in the ruling classes, now, could it? *Self-Help* let the wealthy off the hook. Here in the twenty-first, it continues its pernicious grip on our imaginations.

———————

At this point you may be thinking, "Hmm, well... that's interesting, I suppose, but what does this Smiles guy have to do with the fact that I hate my job? And I'm trying to find the courage to quit?"

In a word: everything.

Because were it not for the long-lingering influence of *Self-Help*, you might not be hesitating at all. You might have already said goodbye to your cubicle mate and put a down payment on that llama farm. As it is, though, you're fighting an idea whose power has only intensified since Smiles's day, steamrolling the cultural landscape. *Self-Help* transformed quitting from just another option to a moral panic. It marked a crucial change in how people looked at their lives, from regarding destiny as the result of a complex array of factors—among them, your forebears' social class and income level, and the physical and intellectual gifts with which we are endowed—to believing that it arises from a single, simple source: individual effort, or lack thereof. We still live with the legacy of Smiles's philosophy, blaming ourselves if we feel frustrated and stuck, wondering why we can't seem to get ahead—and get out of our own way.

Smiles may not be a household name anymore, but the principle of self-help that he championed still controls our expectations for a happy and meaningful life. A fervent belief in self-creation remains a driving force. The burgeoning life coach movement comes right out of the *Self-Help* playbook, so much so that if Smiles were alive at this moment, and willing to swap that frock coat and starched collar for yoga pants and comfy T-shirt, he'd be a life coach himself. Of course, he'd have tough competition for signing up acolytes. In 2007 a woman named Brooke Castillo, anointed as "the reigning queen of the world of life coaching" by the *Guardian*, turned the idea of self-empowerment into a lucrative empire of podcasts, books, and online courses that continues to produce even more life coaches. Her profits quadrupled between 2017 and 2019, the paper reports, and in 2020, Castillo's Life Coach School took in $37 million in gross revenue. Her clients, reports journalist Rachel Monroe, are told that their "problems are not caused by external circumstances—bad bosses, difficult mothers-in-law—but rather their inability to manage their own thoughts."

Yet there's a dark side to this lofty concept of perfectibility. For one thing, it can make us feel inadequate and ashamed if our lives don't measure up to some arbitrary standard of joy and net worth—because couldn't you have worked harder? Really? Come on, now. Admit it.

Even more insidious is its effect on us in times of emotional devastation. As grief counselor Julia Samuel writes in *Grief Works*, "Our culture is imbued with the belief that we can fix just about anything and make it better...Grief is the antithesis of this belief: it eschews avoidance and requires endurance, and forces us to accept that there are some things in this world that simply cannot be fixed."

That's hard to acknowledge in a culture where the goal of infinite perfectibility has wormed its way so deeply into our psyches. Digging it out is difficult—especially, perhaps, for Americans, living as we do in a land where our foundational idea is one of pep and drive and restless optimism. "We are a forward-looking, future-preoccupied people," Sharon O'Brien muses in her introduction to a new edition of Willa Cather's *My Ántonia*, a novel that explores the hardships and perils of the immigrant experience in the American West. "We see this belief...more crudely and opportunistically manipulated in the advertising that caters to our desire for renewal—ads for cosmetics, running shoes, diet products, hair restorers, even kitchen appliances, products that promise a transformed and redeemed self."

———————

Brad Stulberg has seen firsthand the negative results of this endless quest to be flawless. In his recent book, *The Practice of Groundedness: A Transformative Path to Success That Feeds—Not Crushes—Your Soul*, the writer and fitness trainer describes the plight of many high-achieving people he's coached: they're weary and stressed. They run fast every day but don't sense any forward progress. The more they achieve, the emptier they feel. Yet they don't want to quit or even change course, Stulberg tells me, because they believe they'll lose momentum and fall behind.

The culprit, he says, is "heroic individualism," which is "perpetuated by a culture that relentlessly says you need to be better, feel better, think more positively, have more...Many men describe it as a cumbersome need to be bulletproof, invincible. Many women report they must be everything always, constantly falling short of impossible expectations."

 WHITE FLAG MOMENT

On the morning of April 6, 2007, I was lying on the floor of my home office in a pool of blood. On my way down, my head had hit the corner of my desk, cutting my eye and breaking my cheekbone. I had collapsed from exhaustion and lack of sleep...After my fall, I had to ask myself, Was this what success looked like? Was this the life I wanted?...I knew something had to radically change.

—*Arianna Huffington*

The pressure to be a superhuman achiever stretches back a long way in history, Stulberg notes: "It's just wrapped in different paper [today]...It is okay to strive and have ambition, but that striving and ambition must be grounded in values that care for yourself and your community. Otherwise, it becomes extremely destructive. There's no point in reaching a finish line if it makes you miserable and destroys the world along the way. That's just dumb."

We get messages every day, though, that tell us that quitting is unacceptable. Ignore them, he recommends. And think of strategic quitting as an act of heroic resistance: "There are all kinds of external dashboards in life, but it's so helpful to have an internal dashboard, too. I think in a lot of cases that people who quit when they are doing what others would consider well are crushing the external dashboards—and falling on their internal ones. It takes a lot of courage to prioritize your internal dashboard in those situations."

Quitting. Backing away. Recalibrating. All words for the same basic maneuver, for trying to see the world not as a zero-sum game with winners and losers, but as a place where everybody is both, from time to time. For regarding life not as a mountain to be climbed on your own, but as a road to be traveled in the company of others who struggle with the same doubts and sorrows.

As novelist Matthew Specktor puts it in a 2021 interview in *The Millions*:

> Unless one is lying to oneself, life is a hotbed of failure. You miss your goals. Your relationships implode. You lose your job. You disappoint your friends, or your children. You have an experience of illness or loss. This happens. To everybody, it happens.
>
> But with any luck…you are likely to succeed at least occasionally. And if you can internalize some of those successes as effectively as we all do our disappointments… you become a little more flexible. The failures might not torture you as much and the successes won't mess with your head.

Flexibility, though, is not an attribute Smiles prized. He recommended the opposite: rigidity. No wavering, no compromise—and especially no quitting. "Men must necessarily be the active agents of their own well-being," he wrote, adding, "The road of human welfare lies along the old highway of steadfast well-doing." His idea is still around today, in the form of books and articles and webinars and podcasts put out by ministers and mystics, by nutritionists and physicians, by athletes and salespeople and celebrities, by professors and pundits. They deliver variations of the same old message: whatever you do, don't quit.

They quit on page 59.

I don't know who they are or where they live or what they do for a living. I don't know the color of their hair or what kind of car they drive. But I know this:

I know precisely where their hope died—because that's where the underlining stops.

For the first 59 pages of my secondhand copy of *The Purpose-Driven Life* by Rick Warren, purchased for a quarter at a Goodwill store, the previous owner had enthusiastically underlined passages that appealed to them, using a bright orange marker. Thick dashes are slashed across sentences to highlight them. Entire paragraphs are corralled in big swooping circles. You can almost channel the reader's excitement:

This, this, and—oh my, yes! THIS.

Page after page, chapter after chapter, exclamation points bother the margins. The rest of the available white space is scarred with check marks, the symbolic equivalent of a lusty "Heck, yeah!" Every so often a concept from the text is restated across the bottom of the page in my unknown reader's hectic, inspired scribble: *Find out what life is. Find the reason.*

And then—suddenly—it all stops.

On page 59, at the end of chapter 7, my reader is charging hard, writing in an impatient script below the last sentence of the chapter: *Giving ourselves to be used for His purpose.* When the book resumes again with chapter 8, though, and thereafter...

Crickets.

No more exclamation points. No more check marks. No more big circles. No more pithy paraphrases in the margins alongside the book's many bullet points.

For the remainder of the 321 pages (excluding appendices and resource guide), the pages look untouched. There's nary a nick, a smudge, a line, a dot, or a jot. There's not so much as a dried drop of spilled coffee or a random eyelash.

I can guess what happened to this reader (yes, they might have died, but let's go with the most probable explanation):

They quit.

I'm not criticizing this anonymous reader. Far from it. Few people make it all the way through a self-help book, including me, or stick for long with a wellness program. We may start out with the best of intentions but then we stall out and drift away, and when we do, we cringe beneath the weight of a double whammy: not only did we quit, but we quit during a deliberate and premeditated attempt to learn how not to be a quitter.

So how did the poor soul who cracked open *The Purpose-Driven Life*, armed with all those grand hopes and bright expectations, not to mention a sharp-scented, moist-tipped orange marker probably bought in a multipack at Costco, deal with their failure?

For starters, they ditched the evidence. They got the book out of their sight by donating it to a thrift store. Thrift stores, in fact, were my chief hunting grounds for self-help books, old and new, to see what they had to say about quitting. I scoured Goodwills, rooted around in used bookstores, halted my trusty Honda at every yard sale and church rummage sale that caught my eye. Self-help books, I can now report, generally outnumber all other categories in those emporia, easily beating out history and biography and science fiction, handily crushing romance and religion and horror and even cookbooks. To me, that alone proves—and does so rather poignantly—the strength of our evergreen desire to better ourselves, to change what needs to be changed, to be happier and more loving (and, God knows, thinner). But it also suggests how inadequate so many of these books are, and how—like junk food—they often leave us hungrier than we were before we consumed them. And so we keep searching and finding and reading and quoting and quitting, and then we go out and search some more.

But here's the thing: having not paid much attention to them before, I discovered that many self-help books are interesting and thought-provoking and feature a golden optimism at their core. If you're someone who wants to be and do better, that's hard to argue with.

"Critics of self-help," writes Anna Katharina Schaffner, a scholar who studies the genre, complain that it "casts all our problems as personal, and our failures as owing to a lack of willpower and resilience." Yet there's an upside, she reminds us: "The wish to improve ourselves is bound up with our need for self-knowledge, for mastery and for transformation. It is a timeless desire and an essential part of what makes us human."

Wendy Kaminer agrees. She's the author of a witty takedown of the personal transformation movement, *I'm Dysfunctional, You're Dysfunctional: The Recovery Movement and Other Self-Help Fashions*, but she gets the lure of the books that promote it: "People walk around bewildered—it's part of the human condition," she tells me. "It's not hard to understand the appeal of a self-identified expert who says, 'You don't have to be so bewildered. I've got this formula.'" And the formula has a simple main ingredient: don't quit.

———

Today we'd call it manifestation, but in the early twentieth century, it was known as the New Thought movement. The two books that milked it best—and that most passionately vilified quitting—are still around today, sold at sales conventions, slipped into stockings by well-meaning aunts, given as graduation gifts. You've heard of them, even if you haven't seen the actual books: *Think and Grow Rich* and *The Power of Positive Thinking*. The titles alone have a place in American intellectual history. You can draw a line from today's life coaches back to the authors of these books—respectively, Napoleon Hill and Norman Vincent Peale.

The idea behind both: If you visualize what you want, you'll get it. Or as it's sometimes phrased these days on inspirational posters and screen savers featuring snowcapped mountain peaks: If you can dream it, you can do it. All that stands in your way is *you*—and your ability to resist the urge to quit. So get cracking.

"Practical dreamers do not quit!" Hill wrote in his book, first published in 1937 and reprinted multiple times. His introduction claims that the steel magnate Andrew Carnegie taught him the secret to achieving great wealth and lasting personal happiness. (Never mind that Hill, who died in 1970, produced no evidence that he'd ever met Carnegie, and that Carnegie was conveniently dead by the time *Think and Grow Rich* was published, and never mind that the book is replete with unsourced tales about ordinary people who made millions merely because they thought very, very hard about it.) Among the strategies: "Thoughts which are mixed with any of the feelings of emotions constitute a 'magnetic' force which attracts other similar or related thoughts." You can overcome anything—unless you give up, Hill insisted: "No man is ever whipped, until he quits—in his own mind."

In a chapter titled "Persistence," he wrote, "The majority of people are ready to throw their aims and purposes overboard, and give up at the first sign of opposition or misfortune...Lack of persistence is one of the major causes of failure." Not the Great Depression or—in the present century—the implosion of the housing market or rampant inflation. Or, in *any* century, a debilitating injury to a family member and inadequate health insurance coverage. "If one does not possess persistence," Hill lectured, "one does not achieve noteworthy success in any calling."

Hill offered what he called a Persistence Inventory, which asked readers if any of sixteen self-sabotaging behaviors sounded familiar to them, such as "indifference, usually reflected in one's readiness to compromise on all occasions, rather than meet opposition and fight it," and "willingness, even eagerness, to quit at the first sign of defeat."

While *Think and Grow Rich* has the ring of a carnival barker's canny come-on, the book by Peale is gentler and calmer. It's hard to dislike it as much as Hill's, given its kindly, grandfatherly tone, even though the message is much the same: you can think your way into joy and prosperity, into having supportive friends and loving family members. Events don't just happen to you—you summon them into existence. You call them into your life by the quality and direction of your thoughts. Your thoughts are your destiny. So don't even *think* of thinking about quitting.

Both men came to the advice-book game after discovering a gift for public performance: Peale was a minister, Hill a salesman and aspiring actor.

The Power of Positive Thinking begins with a bang: "Believe in yourself! Have faith in your abilities!" The rest of the book is filled with similarly stirring, uplifting prescriptions for behavior: "For the next twenty-four hours," Peale advised, "deliberately speak hopefully about everything, about your job, about your health, about your future."

The original owner of my secondhand copy added only one line in the margin of a single page. It's different from the frenzy of orange-hued comments left by the reader of *The Purpose-Driven Life* (until page 59, that is). This is a quieter response.

When I came across the line, I found myself instantly filling in the backstory, imagining my reader buying the book when it was shiny and new in 1952—perhaps, I thought, the day after some emotional crisis played out in the kitchen after midnight, amid a scattering of broken promises and last chances.

Heartbroken, they had underlined Peale's words in the text: "It is a well-defined and authentic principle that what the mind profoundly expects it tends to receive. Perhaps this is true because what you really expect is what you actually want."

Along the left margin next to that passage my reader had put a tiny hand-drawn star and these words:

*Did I want Ed to leave?

I hope that if they wanted Ed back and he was worthy of their love, he finally returned.

Paul Peterson has never underlined a single passage in any self-help book. He's never circled an insight. He's never turned down the corner of a page for later reference. He's barely *opened* a self-help book, truth be told. He has an aversion to them, especially the kind that people give you because they think you need to read them. It's a little like getting a diet book you didn't ask for: you spend the rest of the day checking out your rump in the hall mirror and worrying.

But even Peterson, no fan of books that offer tidy tips for a happy life, can understand why people buy them: "Rules are good. People need a game plan."

He's had a lot of bad bosses—no, let's use his words: he's had some "egotistical assholes" who made his life a living hell until he could get out of their clutches—but he'll never forget the nasty trick pulled by the one in Modesto, California: he handed Peterson a self-help book.

"It was crap," Peterson tells me flatly. "I looked on the shelf behind him and that guy had every self-help book and tape ever made."

Peterson's umbrage was understandable. He was doing just fine without the tips—because, along with being talented and clever, he'd mastered the strategic power of quitting. In a thirty-five-year career on the air at a series of radio stations, moving to progressively bigger markets with progressively bigger paychecks, he always quit on a dime when a better offer came along. And better offers were always coming along.

"I had an unrealistic belief in myself," he tells me with a laugh. "And I could never quite settle on anything, on what I really wanted to do." So he just kept moving. And prospered.

Born and raised in Mesa, Arizona, Peterson had two passions growing up: listening to baseball games on the radio and listening to rock music on the radio. The common denominator—radio—became his life's work.

"I loved it. I had a blast," declares Peterson, who now lives in Phoenix. His most memorable night was December 8, 1980. "I was on the air the night John Lennon was assassinated. The whole world went crazy. People were calling the station and crying."

He quickly developed a distinctive presence on the air, aided by a scimitar-sharp wit. "I moved up the food chain very fast. Along the way, I became pretty pragmatic about my career." He worked at stations in Phoenix, then California and in many cities in the Midwest, including Chicago.

Ironically, given his general disdain for the genre, he has a family connection to the self-development business. "My uncle was a very famous self-help guy." His father's sister was the first wife of Earl Nightingale, a popular radio personality in the 1960s and '70s whose syndicated show offered motivational bromides in a pleasingly rough-edged baritone. Nightingale, who died in 1989, expanded his empire into books and tapes, crediting the ideas in *Think and Grow Rich* with inspiring him to get into the self-help game.

Peterson is fairly certain that his famous uncle would've had some stern words for him about all the quitting. But quitting was essential to his own success, Peterson says; it was another tool, another way to climb the ladder: "I wanted something really big in life." Broadcasting was a perfect way to achieve that because, he concludes with a chuckle, "I never had an indoor voice."

     WHITE FLAG MOMENT

One day the boss called me in and started critiquing my copy. I was being abused. I just blew. I said, "You can't do what I do." I pointed to the people outside his office. "No one out there can do what I do." I was sitting and then I got animated and I stood up to make my points. It was like the floodgates opened. I went back to my desk and I finished my shift. Came home and sent a one-sentence email: "I won't be back."

—Paul Peterson

Ron and Rick have never met. Chances are, they never will. They live almost a thousand miles apart. Their only connection is that each talked to me about the many times he's changed direction. They have very different views of quitting and the effect it can have upon a life.

One of them sees quitting as an anchor. The other sees it as a sail.

Ron Rhoden is a self-described seeker. Several shelves in the home he shares with his wife and their two dogs on the outskirts of a small Midwestern town are filled with self-help books, from which he can quote with ease. He often peruses YouTube videos on his phone and listens to podcasts produced by self-help authors.

"My whole life has been a soul search," he tells me. "I've always had this longing that I've tried to fulfill. I've never managed to do that. If I had to say why I've quit so many jobs, it's because I don't find them fulfilling."

Knowing that I want to talk to him about quitting, he's dug out some old resumes to show me. "They go back to 1986. I had forgotten about a lot of these jobs—that's how many I've had."

A partial list: he's been a photographer at an amusement park and at Walmart; a cook at McDonald's and later in a diner; a factory worker; an electrician; a ballroom dancing instructor; a masseuse; a help-desk representative for a computer company; a delivery person for bottled water in office buildings; a bartender; an over-the-road truck driver; a real estate salesperson; an auctioneer. Some of his jobs have been entrepreneurial—he's built and sold canoes and coffee tables.

"I wish I'd stuck with some of the earlier jobs," he says. "I think I'd be in a better position today."

 WHITE FLAG MOMENT

When I think about why I quit so often, the thing that hits me in the face is—I never wanted to be what everybody else was. That's my driving force. I wanted to be different. I never had any interest in being an ordinary person.

—Ron Rhoden

The range of his skills and experiences, I point out, is amazing. He didn't fail at those positions; he chose to quit and move on. Employers were sorry to see him go. They'd take him back in a flash. But many of his self-help books and videos would put the blame for his discontent right there: on leaving a lot of jobs.

Is quitting really a career killer? Is having a variety of jobs such a bad thing? According to a 2021 article in *Inc.*, that's a hard no. "There's no need for a mad rush to find the ideal job," says an executive coach quoted in the piece. "The first part...of your career is testing multiple jobs." Quitting for something better—or maybe just something different—should be the norm, not the aberration.

In a survey conducted by LinkedIn that asked users to come up with the advice they'd give their twenty-year-old selves, "the same advice came up again and again," the article states, summarized by phrases such as "continue testing," "make mistakes and keep learning," and "don't be afraid to explore." The bottom line, *Inc.* advised, is this: "The best way to figure out your career is through action."

Maybe it's not so much the quitting we need to avoid. Maybe it's the negative associations *about* the quitting that society insists upon.

———

Rick McVey has jumped from job to job, too, but that hopscotching history doesn't trouble him. It delights him: "Every time I quit something, it was the right decision at that point in my life," he tells me. "I do like change."

He recently moved from River Forest, Illinois, to Mobile, Alabama. "My best friend lives in New Orleans. I'd go down several times a year and she and I would go on road trips. We went to Mobile once and just kept going back. The more I went, the more I liked it."

Born in Lancaster, Pennsylvania, McVey grew up in nearby York, where his father worked in a Caterpillar tractor plant. That was McVey's first job, too, during his senior year in high school.

Later they put him in a management training program and sent him to Cleveland—and then came a long succession of jobs and cities and adventures. When something more promising came along, he'd grab it. He ran a men's clothing store for a time, and when one of his employees gave notice and said he was going to nursing school, McVey thought, "Nursing school. *Hmm…*"

After graduating from nursing school at forty, he worked as an ICU nurse for three years. Then it was off to Louisville to help run clinical trials for a new AIDS treatment, followed by stints in several cities in Illinois to work in cardiovascular departments. And don't forget his years as a pharmaceutical salesperson, which took him to a different city every few days.

"I loved it," McVey recalls. "Miami on Monday. Wednesday—San Diego."

But when he'd worked at that job long enough, he had another *hmm* moment and considered buying a B and B. "It sounded like too much work, though."

Instead, he bought a flower shop in the Lincoln Park neighborhood of Chicago. He ran it for five years. "We had amazing clients—Bob Dylan, Sheryl Crow, Michelle Obama, Venus and Serena Williams."

He was in a relationship for two decades but it ended amicably. His former partner, McVey says, "recently told me that he admired me because I could move to a totally different city and immediately have a whole life."

Jobs aren't the only things he regularly quits. He'd been a Presbyterian for a time and was ordained as a deacon in the church. He mulled over the idea of becoming a Catholic but ultimately decided upon the Episcopal church. Now it's Judaism that calls to him. "I took eighteen weeks of classes" before converting, he says.

The move to Mobile was intended as a retirement adventure, but he's considering getting his real estate license. More *hmm*s, that is, may lie ahead: "It's on to the next challenge."

Do people ever tell him he quits too often?

Never. "I find that when I share my story with people, they're inspired. Sometimes I hear people say, 'I hate getting old.' I say to them, 'Oh, it's never been better!'"

Quitting is a liberating force, he believes, and it's also a healthy habit that's right up there with eating more leafy greens and making time for morning meditation. It helps keep his mind, body, and soul more limber: "I have never been happier or more content in my whole life than I am right now."

PERMISSION SLIP

You've been told since you were a child that perseverance is the key to success. You've read books and listened to podcasts and watched YouTube videos that claim quitting's bad. But viewed from another angle, the picture of quitting gets more complicated: It is, after all, a way to start fresh. To draw a line between who you are and who you want to be. It's not about a lack of focus—it's about a sense of infinite possibility.

Chapter Five

Luck and Letting Go: Things. Just. Happen.

Fundamental randomness is unbearable to us...
We don't give up until we find comfort in settling
on some cause, no matter how implausible it might
be. And now, suddenly, quantum physics tells us
of events that just happen. Einstein was disturbed
by this. He supposedly once exclaimed that if
randomness remained with us, he would sooner
work in a casino than as a physicist.

—*Anton Zeilinger*

Sharon Harvey won't take the credit. A bold and fearless act of quitting permanently changed her life for the better—not to mention the lives of hundreds of homeless dogs and stray cats—but she's convinced that it wasn't really her doing at all.

Chalk it up instead, she says, to two powerful and mysterious entities.

The first one: luck.

The second: Hugh.

We'll get to the luck part in a moment, but first, who's Hugh and how did he change the life of a woman who, until 2003, was the manager of the vascular medicine department at Cleveland Clinic, a world-renowned medical facility, a position of enormous responsibility (not to mention prestige and excellent salary), for almost twenty years?

"I'd never walked into an animal shelter before 2000," Harvey tells me. That was the year she decided to volunteer at one near her home in a Cleveland suburb. Among her first assignments was to train a dog named Hugh. "He'd been found in horrible shape near a dumpster. He was really, really sick. But he had a spark, a zest to live. And incredible courage. He was plain brown. Big and fluffy and brown. But as wonderful as they come. There wasn't a lot of flair to Hugh. He was just a solid, devoted animal. But when he bonded to you, he bonded hard and strong."

After she adopted Hugh, she began spending more and more of her time at the shelter, helping with the care and feeding of other Hughs. When the paid director's job came open, Harvey was—to her infinite surprise—intrigued. She had a decision to make.

On the one hand, there was her long and fulfilling career at Cleveland Clinic.

On the other hand, there was . . . Hugh.

"I credit him for giving me the courage to make such a big, honking career shift. I'm not a risk taker. I don't love change. And I was going to have to take a significant pay cut and cut in benefits."

But if you've ever had a dog that you loved beyond all logic and reason, and if you've ever gazed into their eyes and saw therein the spirit of all lost and large-souled dogs awaiting rescue, you know which option Harvey chose. "I thought, 'I can go with what's safe and secure and makes sense. Or take a chance for once on my passion.'" So she quit the sure thing.

After running her local shelter for a few years, she took the top job at the Cleveland Animal Protective League, where she now leads a seventy-person staff and administers a $6.5 million annual budget.

Leaving her job at Cleveland Clinic wasn't the first time she'd quit something important—just the first time she'd done so and never looked back. She was in the second class of women admitted to the US Coast Guard Academy, the class of 1981. But she hadn't bargained on the sexism and harassment, she says, and resigned before graduation. "To the consternation of my family, whom I'd never disappointed in my life, I left after two years. And there are times I wonder if I should've sucked it up and stuck it out."

Not once, however, has she doubted the wisdom of her switch from the world of providing care for two-legged animals to the world of saving the four-legged kind: "Not a single regret. *Ever.*"

She'll be forever grateful to Hugh for helping her make the leap. But there was another factor in the mix, along with Hugh's undeniable charm: the fortunate fluke. The thing that Thomas Wolfe called "that dark miracle of chance which makes new magic in a dusty world."

Harvey knows that she and Hugh might never have met. "There was definitely luck involved. I'm not the bravest person in the world. I was in the right place at the right time. Certain things had to fall into place when they did. I'm not sure I would've plotted this out on my own—if the opportunity hadn't hit me in the head."

So what if Hugh had never come into her life? What would have happened then?

She has no idea. Nobody does, about their own path or anybody else's. It's the kind of thing we tend to think about late at night when we can't fall asleep: *What would've happened if...?* And the fact that we ask ourselves that kind of question reveals a lot about why we don't quit things more often—and maybe why we should.

———————

This is not exactly breaking news, but here goes:

Life is ridiculously random and infuriatingly inscrutable. Deserving and honorable people sometimes fail while lowlife scumbags rise to the top. Life, to say the least, isn't fair.

I can hear your question from here: *Hold on, Julia. If everybody knows that* already—*which they do*—*then why are you repeating it and why can't we just hear more about the adventures of that big brown dog instead?*

Because the unpredictability of our fates is one of those prickly little truths that we try earnestly to deny, a denial that figures prominently in how we deal with quitting. We much prefer to pretend that we're calling the shots in our lives. That we make our own decisions. That what happens to us is a direct result of our choices and, as Samuel Smiles would insist, of the amount of work we put in and the number of sacrifices we make toward reaching our goals. That we'll succeed—if we don't quit first.

It's a sweet idea. And it's also baloney.

We are, inevitably, at the mercy of circumstance. And circumstance doesn't give a toss about our dreams or our well-being. Or whether we toiled and sweated and endured—or kicked back and painted our toenails with hot-pink polish. Whether we're kind and thoughtful or selfish and obnoxious.

Because Things. Just. Happen.

That randomness can cut both ways—try checking in with any dog or cat recently adopted from the animal shelter Harvey runs. (The gratitude in their eyes for getting off the streets and enjoying regular meals will overcome the language barrier.) Sometimes chance brings wonderful results. Sometimes not.

What if the person who found a shivering, starving Hugh beside the dumpster that day had gone down another alley instead and Hugh wasn't rescued in time?

So life's a crapshoot. And we all *know* it's a crapshoot. But the message imparted in books that promise to improve you is precisely the opposite. It assures us that we're in unconditional charge of our lives.

There's a perfectly sound reason for that, of course: telling people that their existence doesn't matter very much in an unfathomably vast universe, that chaos reigns and pain is inevitable, that no matter how many hours you spend meditating each morning or how many positive affirmations you repeat or how many kale-crammed diets or draconian exercise programs you undertake, a certain number of bad things are going to happen to you *just because* is not widely regarded as a great motivator. It's also not a recommended sales pitch for a self-help podcast or plant-based meal-delivery service.

Thus, we gratefully welcome the fiction—even though we know better—that we're running the show because it's a more pleasing concept to embrace than the alternative, which is helpless victimhood. We'd rather not acknowledge the unsettling truth about life's essential randomness.

Better to chalk up an undesirable outcome to the fact that you— or even better, somebody else, because then you can be satisfyingly judgmental—made a lousy choice than to acknowledge that often we don't have much say over what happens to us, no matter *what* we choose. That we can do our absolute best—and sometimes, it doesn't matter.

Because Things. Just. Happen. All the time. Everywhere.

Things you didn't cause. Things you can't change. Things like divorce and volcanoes. Accidents and anomalies. Things you didn't want to happen but that happened anyway. Or things that you did.

Things you don't see coming but that, for good or for ill, forever alter the course of your life once they arrive.

We know this—but we don't *want* to know it. And so we resist it by falling for the idea that promises the opposite, that tells us that we're the one in the captain's chair, the catbird seat, the queen's throne. An idea that claims we hold the tiller, the joystick, the whip hand. An idea that assures us that we have power and choice.

In *Thinking, Fast and Slow*, his incisive study of the incongruities of human cognition, Daniel Kahneman points to "a puzzling limitation of our mind: our excessive confidence in what we believe we know, and our apparent inability to acknowledge the full extent of our ignorance and the uncertainty of the world we live in. We are prone to overestimate how much we understand the world and to underestimate the role of chance in human events. Overconfidence is fed by the illusory certainty of hindsight."

If we're honest, we'll admit that we all try to maintain the myth of individual autonomy until we just can't swing it anymore, until we're confronted by a life-altering situation not of our making: We're diagnosed with a disease we've never even heard of. We suffer the death of a loved one. Or lesser blows: A friend lets us down. We're passed over for a promotion.

Or—because the Great Cosmic Coin Flip can come up heads just as readily as tails—we celebrate a new baby, a new job, a new romance, or a green light and no traffic when we're running late for an appointment. Up or down, success or failure—it can go either way, which is both exhilarating and terrifying.

So we have to find a way to rise above the randomness, to deal with accidents and happenstance. Lest we be permanently discouraged, constantly disillusioned, or otherwise victimized by those vicissitudes, we must learn to exercise the one small bit of dominion that we *do* have, to snatch at the last fragile thread of control in a world that always seems to be rapidly unraveling right before our eyes.

Traditionally, the advice we hear is to grit our teeth and grab hold of whatever's handy, as though the rules to achieving success and joy are the same as surviving our turn on a mechanical bull. But I'd like to offer a different suggestion:

Give up.

———————

On September 7, 2009, Dan Cnossen stepped on a land mine while on patrol in Afghanistan as a Navy SEAL. Awakening from a medically induced coma a week and a day later at Walter Reed National Military Medical Center, he learned the extent of his injuries: above-the-knee amputations of both legs, broken pelvis, grievous internal injuries. He would have to undergo more than two dozen surgeries. The only way he made it through his ordeal, Cnossen told the *Washington Post* in a 2022 interview, was by using a technique he'd mastered during his SEAL training.

In a nutshell, he quit.

He had to let go of lofty, abstract, overarching goals—because they seemed distant, fuzzy, impossibly unreachable, and hence, dispiriting. He had to abandon the path he'd envisioned for his life and find—or forge—another one.

"It helps to have long-term goals, but what you really need are short-term goals to focus on. I needed to get through every day," Cnossen told the *Post*. He'd used a similar technique to master the aptly named Hell Week, the legendarily rigorous SEAL training. Instead of proclaiming an overall goal, he realized that "the better strategy . . . was to make it to the end of the specific task at hand." No grand slogans, no soaring, inspirational quotations—and no looking past the moment at hand. Just quiet, steady, incremental progress. He quit the big thing in order to embrace the small thing—and in the end, the accumulation of small things *became* the big thing: rebuilding his life.

Cnossen, who won a gold medal in the men's sitting skiing biathlon event at the 2018 Paralympic Winter Games, didn't know that an explosion was going to rip off his legs while he served his country. But faced with the challenge of catastrophic injury, he had to give up one way of life and take hold of another. At times, that meant just getting to the end of a day—or the end of an hour.

He didn't choose his fate. But he chose how he would respond to it: with courage and grace.

Others, too, have faced ordeals that were devastating in physical and emotional ways. They, too, had to make a distinction between what they couldn't change and what they could—and if they decided that a particular challenge fell into the latter category, to go out and change it. Many times, that means quitting.

———

"The lesson I learned is that you don't always have control over what happens to you. All you can control is how you spend your time. Are you learning? Are you growing?"

That's Michele Weldon, an intense, dynamic woman who lives in a Chicago suburb. She's published six books—she's just finishing up her seventh—and too many essays to keep track of. She taught at Northwestern University for almost two decades and now mentors writers who are finding their voices.

She found hers after a traumatizing personal experience. It wasn't what she'd wanted for her life—it wasn't what *anybody* would want—but it happened, and she had to deal with it. Among the ways she did that was to realize it wasn't her fault. And that she had the power to change things—and the responsibility to pass along to others a crucial, often overlooked truth:

Quitting is always an option.

"For nine years I was married to a charismatic, successful lawyer who everybody thought was marvelous—but he was physically and emotionally abusive," she tells me. "In marriage counseling, I was always trying to fix it. And then I came to the revelation—'You can't fix this.'"

Still, she hung on, mostly for the sake of their three young sons. Leaving her marriage and living as a single mom would be a last resort, an overwhelmingly big step, directly into unfamiliar territory.

"I'd never quit anything before. I always felt I could change the situation. Make it better. And endure it. I'd seen the stats. I knew the outlook financially and emotionally for fatherless sons. So I thought, 'I have to exhaust every possible remedy.'"

Finally, after grappling with doubt and self-blame, but with the tensions escalating again between her and her husband, she decided in 1986 to seek an end to the marriage. It was, she recalls, a shattering, I-can't-believe-I'm-really-doing-this kind of moment.

Friends tried to be supportive, but internal messages can sometimes shout down the ones that are coming from the outside: "They'd say, 'Oh, that's so courageous.' And I'd say to myself, '*Was* it? Or was it stupid?'"

Weldon decided to put her uncertainty and fear into words, hoping the process would be therapeutic. First step: she wrote an essay about her experiences for a writing competition and won the top prize. That essay became the opening chapter of her first memoir, *I Closed My Eyes*. "It was the first time I told the truth to myself. And I told it out loud."

WHITE FLAG MOMENT

Women like me who care for children and sometimes elderly parents and homes and careers—sometimes we want to do one less thing…Sometimes we are so tired of being together and in charge, we do not even want to talk, listen, or pick out a movie…Sometimes we want to melt quietly for a little bit before we go right back to being CEO of the family corporation.

—*Michele Weldon*

Quitting, once unthinkable, now is a strategy she's able to employ at will, she tells me. A family tragedy—the death of her beloved brother, Paul, from cancer in 2021—brought home to her once again the creative and life-affirming power of quitting. There was nothing she could have done to save her brother, but she can use his life as a reminder to forgive herself for things outside of her control—and to use the things she *can* control, like her time and her emotional energy, in positive ways.

"After my brother's death I began editing friendships and relationships much more carefully. I've quit relationships that are stale and not uplifting. That is very freeing—walking away from things.

"I just ask myself, 'Do I really want to spend my time doing that?'"

Like Weldon, Amy Dickinson had to learn how to quit. For her, too, the events that prompted the lesson were not of her making. They were, by and large, things that just happened to her, things she'd have given anything in the world never to have experienced. But once she discovered the power of quitting, Dickinson tells me, she realized just what a positive, life-affirming, healing force it can be.

You've probably heard her quick-witted contributions to *Wait Wait...Don't Tell Me!*, the National Public Radio quiz show on which she's a regular panelist. Or nodded in agreement at her thoughtful, funny, no-nonsense replies to readers' questions in her nationally syndicated advice column. Or read her two best-selling memoirs, *The Mighty Queens of Freeville* and *Strangers Tend to Tell Me Things*.

Dickinson comes across as an accomplished, unflappable woman, brimming with confidence and optimism. But she wasn't always that way, she says.

"The short version is that my father left our family extremely abruptly, leaving four kids, a farm in foreclosure, and a barn full of Holstein cows that needed milking twice a day. Talk about a quitter!" Later, "my first husband walked away—again very abruptly. Again with the quitting! So—as someone who got quit on a couple of times in very big ways—I have wrestled mightily with this."

As a result, she says, she became the opposite of a quitter: Convinced that "quitting is losing," she turned herself into a driven, conscientious, ultra-reliable person who never gave up on anything—or anyone. But then came the moment in 2020 when she resigned from the Daughters of the American Revolution—a turning point in her life that we'll discuss in chapter 11. "I tried quitting for the first time in my life, and I feel completely liberated."

The key, Dickinson advises, is to let go of other people's expectations and to do as your own heart and moral compass tell you to do. "Without question, I don't think we quit often enough. I know *I* don't," she declares. "Americans have the reputation lately of being entitled and undisciplined, but I do think that baked into our cultural DNA is this sense of shame when you want to stop or withdraw from an obligation.

"But I believe that if you deliberately quit something you don't enjoy, it frees up space for you to take on something else. Or to lie on the couch. Or to exercise your own free will to spend your own time on things you enjoy."

———————

Christine Broquet never saw it coming.

She had been married for twenty-three years. Her life wasn't perfect—she and her husband, Bernie, had definitely grown apart, and he spent a great deal of time abroad for his job—but they were always cordial and respectful toward each other. Their kids, Zoe, then sixteen, and Remy, eleven, were terrific.

So things were fine.

Except that they weren't. Not really.

She found out just how *not* fine they actually were when, during a marriage counseling session, her husband revealed that he intended to transition to female.

"I was in denial," recalls Broquet, who lives in the Chicago area. "I was, 'We can work this out.' I wasn't willing to give up."

But her determination not to quit didn't matter anymore. It wasn't her decision. Her husband wanted a divorce. Matters had been taken out of her hands. She had to focus on her children—and make sure they were okay, after the earthquake that had rocked the family.

They were. Both now have their own families and careers they love. Broquet is thrilled to be a grandmother. But the memory of the day in 2002 when her then-husband delivered that emotional bombshell still haunts her. It took her a while to understand that agreeing to end the marriage was the right decision—even though that hadn't been her first instinct. She'd been ready to fight for her family. To not give up. Only gradually did she see that giving up was what she needed to do. She'd tried her best. This wasn't her fault. But that didn't make it hurt any less.

"Until my marriage blew up in this bizarre way," she says, "nothing bad had ever happened to me."

 WHITE FLAG MOMENT

Usually, I don't quit things. I stay and I suffer! But one day I was at my job. I'd decided I was really tired of being in design. I wanted to be in marketing. My boss called me in and said they were going to give that job to someone else...It was January. We'd had this huge snowfall. And there was a gigantic mound of dirty snow right outside her window. It looked like a beast. I remember looking at that thing and thinking, "I wish that beast would come through that window and bite this woman's head off." That was it for me. I knew I wouldn't be there much longer.

—Christine Broquet

Broquet has worked many years in graphic design. She's writing a memoir about the demise of her marriage—the tentative title is *The Other Woman*—and trying to get to know herself better. It took her a long time, she says, to realize how being blindsided by divorce has affected her ability to speak up for herself in other aspects of her life.

"I've avoided major life decisions because I was traumatized by the marriage," she admits. "A lot of my problems with quitting come from a fear of even trying. I don't quit things very often because I don't *start* things very often."

She's determined to change that. The way to get comfortable with quitting, she says, is to do more so that she'll have more to quit.

———————

Howard Berkes, too, had to quit strategically in order to realize his dreams. He worked hard and took risks, yes, but he also developed a healthy appreciation for the accidents of fate—like, say, erupting volcanoes—that can change anyone's life at any moment.

For his long and award-winning career with National Public Radio that lasted almost four decades, Berkes owes a debt of gratitude to that natural disaster. It was entirely out of his hands, as volcanoes tend to be—but the part of it that *was* in his control, he made the most of.

If you'd wanted to find Berkes back in the late 1970s and early '80s, your best bet would be to head off to the woods in Oregon or Minnesota. That's where a restless, questing Berkes liked to hang out, exploring on his own or leading Outward Bound canoe trips. He'd been a buyer for a university bookstore, a community organizer, a sign language interpreter, and a bunch of other things as he tried to figure out how best to channel his energy and commitment to social justice issues. He'd enrolled in communication classes at a community college, but it wasn't a priority. Far more to his liking, Berkes tells me, was reporting in the field; by that time, he'd begun filing stories as a freelancer at the NPR member station in Eugene.

In the early spring of 1980, Mount Saint Helens, a volcano just south of Seattle, "began to burp and rumble and spit ash," he recalls. "And I filed as many stories and news spots as NPR would take. I became the network's volcano guy." His NPR editor told him to get on the mountain and stay on the mountain.

"But first I had to deal with the prospect of missing classes. I went to a couple of my instructors, explained the situation, and offered to write papers and make presentations on my real-world experiences to make up for lost classes. 'No,' I was told. 'If you miss three classes, you flunk.'" So he quit college.

"And then I got my ass up to that mountain. And I talked my way into the press pool. The experience was epic and resulted in my first live interview on *All Things Considered*."

When the volcano's major eruption occurred on May 18, "that NPR editor made me the primary reporter for network coverage. I was on the air for months."

At year's end, he was hired full-time as one of NPR's first national reporters—even though he'd been told by a boss at his local NPR station that they'd never take somebody who lacked a college degree.

It was the perfect gig for Berkes, who was entranced from the get-go by "the adrenaline and the creative challenge of radio."

———————

A volcano was the catalyst for Berkes's career, but he didn't personally make it erupt. Weldon didn't want to be a single mother. Cnossen didn't choose his horrific injuries. Dickinson didn't ask to have a deadbeat dad and an absent husband. Broquet was blindsided by her ex-husband's announcement that he was transitioning. Each met the challenges that were dished out to them—but they hadn't seen them coming.

A large portion of our lives is beyond our control. We have no say over where we're born, or to whom, or, on so many occasions, which events happen to us and when. The late Justus Rosenberg, who risked his life to work with the French resistance during World War II, once told an interviewer, "There are no geniuses, really, only what people make with what they are given—that, and a confluence of circumstances."

US Senator Bob Dole, who died in 2021, was seriously injured in the line of duty in World War II. In his political career, he came very close to his ultimate goal of the White House. His fate often was a matter of random factors, a point of which George F. Will took note in his column after Dole's passing: "If he had been a few yards away from where he was on that Italian hill on April 14, 1945, or if the war in Europe had ended 25 days earlier, he would have escaped the severe wound that left him in pain the rest of his years. A few thousand more Ohio and Mississippi votes in 1976 would have made Dole vice president."

So we hang on as best we can while we're whirled about by events and contingencies. And within all of that flux and churn and uncertainty, within that constant maelstrom, there's very little we can do. Except this:

We can quit when we need to. And we can let other people quit when *they* need to as well, without judging them.

And those two acts—simple as they sound—just might change the world.

PERMISSION SLIP

You've had some good luck in your life. And some rotten luck, too. It's the same for everyone. Yet within the muddled uncertainty of life, you can perform at least one pure, definitive act: quitting. You can change course when you need to. It's a way of fighting back against random chance—and reclaiming your power.

Chapter Six

Making a Better World—One "I Quit" at a Time

The flip side of positivity is thus a harsh insistence on personal responsibility: if your business fails or your job is eliminated, it must be because you didn't try hard enough.

—*Barbara Ehrenreich*

On January 9, 2022, a fire tore through a high-rise apartment building in the Bronx, killing nineteen people. Children as young as four were among the dead. Citing the fire department's report that a space heater had caused the blaze and that open stairwell doors had helped it to spread, New York City's newly minted mayor, Eric Adams, said, "If we take one message from this," it would be a simple one: "Close the door. Close the door. Close the door."

That enraged journalist Ross Barkan. In an essay titled "Why Is New York City's Mayor Blaming Tenants for the Deadliest Fire in a Century?," Barkan writes, "The story of the Bronx blaze is not one of personal responsibility. By blaming individual actors, Adams instead allows the true culprits off the hook: the building owners. Why did a tenant need to use a space heater? Why were the doors so faulty?"

Thus, some responses to the tragedy were based on a familiar script: tell people at the lower end of the economic ladder that their setbacks are, in large part, of their own making. If only they'd worked harder—and remembered to shut a door—they wouldn't be poor and unlucky and fall victim to a horrific fire. If only they hadn't quit so often.

Barkan, seething at the implication that the tenants were responsible for their own fate, adds in his essay, "More children and adults obsessing over their alleged culpability in crumbling apartment towers will mean a real estate investor class that gets to keep doing what it has always done: cut corners to drive profits."

City officials didn't quote Samuel Smiles, but they might as well have. Because they offered an echo of Smiles's manifesto: if you live on life's margins, if you're falling behind, if bad things happen to you and you wonder why, look in the mirror.

Could there be a connection between our indifference to economic inequality and our celebration of grit?

———————

From fires to foreclosures, from poverty to pandemics, the world is awash in a complex array of problems. The cult of perseverance offers a simple solution: Hang on. Don't quit. But it's a false promise, and in the end, it may make us less compassionate to those in need.

"Self-improvement books do not work. *They do not work.* The whole construct is an illusion," declares McGee, an author and scholar, from her home in New York. "You are *not* an independent self. You're part of a system of organization in which we are all a part. The idea that we're acting as individuals—on a good day, it's hilarious. On a bad day, it's tragic."

McGee's 2005 book, *Self-Help, Inc.: Makeover Culture in American*

Life, offers a sharply argued, cogent critique of personal development programs, especially as they relate to women. I wondered if she'd mellowed in the seventeen years since her book was published.

Fortunately, the answer is no. She's still as skeptical as ever about the promotion of perseverance, but now she has two new reasons to question it (not that a feminist critique wasn't reason enough): the rise of disability studies, a new focus of her research and teaching at Fordham University; and the effect of the pandemic on all of us.

"Self-improvement culture is disembodied," she tells me. "It's a disavowal of our physical vulnerability. One is always supposed to be overcoming one's bodily insufficiency." Self-help pushes "the idea of boundless capacity, with no chinks in the armor." But the Covid-19 virus reminded us all of what people who deal with a disability— their own or that of a loved one—have known all along: no one is exempt from the stark lottery of illness. "People fall," McGee declares. "They have to spend a year in bed. Or they have a child with a developmental disability. We need to do what self-help *doesn't* do—to deal with the body in its frailty, not its capacity. The mind in its feebleness, not its robustness."

Those fawning, they-hit-it-big-so-why-can't-you profiles of billionaires only make matters worse. "Self-help offers this phantasmic ideal of human beings as invincible—the Jeff Bezos ideal. The myth of doing it on our own. Well, imagine if you're on minimum wage and don't have enough money to pay your rent."

In stories about Bill Gates, Mark Zuckerberg, and Elon Musk, the theme is generally the same: They're determined and relentless. They endured setbacks and kept going. They never gave up. If other people struggle and falter—why, it must be because they lack that zeal, that willingness to buckle down and ignore discouragement. Never mind if those who struggle happen to have been born poor, or Black or brown, or female, or with physical or psychological disabilities, or to undocumented parents: all of that can be overcome with enough drive—or so this theory goes.

It's easy to blame people for their own troubles when you're convinced they brought those troubles on themselves by giving up. "The ideal of individual success and self-invention, epitomized in figures such as Benjamin Franklin, Andrew Carnegie, and Bill Gates serves to cajole American workers," McGee writes in *Self-Help, Inc.*

In 2021, the richest people in the country got a whole lot richer. "The past year [was] the best time in history to be one of America's billionaires," wrote Eli Saslow in the *Washington Post*. "Their cumulative wealth has grown by an estimated 70 percent since the beginning of the pandemic...Together, those 745 billionaires are now worth more than the bottom 60 percent of American households combined." That's not a healthy state of affairs—and yet we put up with it. Could there be a link between our cultural bias against quitting and our tolerance of the widening gap between rich and poor? That bias helps us rationalize doing nothing about income inequality: *Those people living in that crappy little house must be lazy. They gotta be quitters. 'Cause everybody knows that success is a matter of gritting it out and believing in yourself.*

We need to devote ourselves, McGee says, to creating a world that works for rich and poor alike: "The goal isn't about the self. The goal is engagement with the world and with other people. We know there's a better way of living and we know that the better way takes one out of 'fixing up' or bolstering the self and into a care for the future. Everyone's future."

———

Phillip Martin doesn't much like the word "perseverance," even though a lot of people might say his life reflects an abundance of that very quality. "It's in the same category as 'Pull yourself up by your bootstraps' type of language," he tells me. "It's overly simplistic and steeped in individualism." He prefers to credit his success to other factors: a great support network—and strategic quitting.

"I've had several major quits in my life," he says, such as withdrawing from college in 1973 to become an activist for racial justice in Boston, a decision that meant he had to leave his hometown of Detroit. "It was the smartest two quits in my life because it altered my future in ways I never could have imagined."

 WHITE FLAG MOMENT

It was April in the spring of 1975. I was sitting in a classroom at Wayne State University. A friend handed me a flyer imploring students to come to Boston that summer "to fight against racism"...That June I drove from Detroit to Boston in a beige Ford Pinto that broke down twice en route. I settled into a home on Waldeck Street in Dorchester with four roommates. For part of the summer, I taught writing and Black history to youngsters at Roxbury's Highland Park Free School.

—*Phillip Martin*

Martin, a senior investigative reporter for WGBH, Boston's National Public Radio station, says the word "perseverance" implies that he's achieved things solely through his own efforts. "The down parts of my ups and downs were temporary because I had a lot of help getting back up," including the support of his wife, Bianca; his mother, Louise; editors at NPR who believed in him early in his career; and teachers and mentors along the way, the people who looked at a young Black man from an impoverished background and saw the accomplished journalist he would become.

To chalk up his success solely to grit is misleading, Martin says. It ignores the role other people have played in his life as he followed his dreams. "I moved to Boston and imagined one day writing about Boston in all its grime, crime, and racial complexity—and that is what I still do."

And he's able to do it not only because he works hard, which he does, or because he's smart and talented, which he is, but also because he had help. When he made big changes such as leaving his hometown, he could count on the love and support of others. He never forgets that. It was an ensemble, Martin says. Not a solo act.

There was a time, Joe Rodriguez recalls, when the future was the last thing in the world he wanted to think about. Born in East Los Angeles to Mexican-American parents who spoke little English—neither his mother nor his father had finished high school—initially he didn't know what he wanted to do with his life. That aimlessness felt like a burden. Like a judgment on his worth as a person.

"It was embarrassing," he tells me. "Not having a set plan, a goal, a job with a regular paycheck."

Lacking a checklist of ambitions and the steps he'd undertake to achieve them, he sensed the world's reproach, Rodriguez says. He was proud of his heritage and didn't want his flailing to reflect badly on the people he loved. As part of an extended family that had come to the United States from northern Mexico, he knew that much was expected of him because of his intelligence and his creativity. But he couldn't seem to steady himself, to take hold.

"I spent five years—in and out, in and out—going to community college. I don't know how many times I changed my major. I was indecisive and insecure." He chuckles. "I let my hair grow long and rode my motorcycle with my friends up and down the California coast." Then he gets somber again. "I was a confused, anchorless kid who couldn't figure out what he wanted to do." Quitting was just about the only thing he did consistently, he says.

During one of his repeat forays to college, he was sitting in the library one day when it struck him: he wanted to be a writer. And to hell with anybody else's opinion about it. "I remember thinking, 'Well, getting a job as a writer will be a fifty-fifty proposition.'"

The gamble paid off. In 2016, Rodriguez retired after nearly three decades in journalism, with columnist jobs at the *Hartford Courant* and the San Jose *Mercury News*. He now lives in a small community near California's San Bernardino Mountains.

Writing a column for a daily newspaper was his dream job. "I liked to center my column on ordinary people." By "ordinary" he doesn't mean unimportant. He means people who aren't celebrities or politicians or business tycoons. People who, like a certain restless, long-haired kid riding a motorcycle up Highway 101 some years ago, may be a little uncertain and even kind of lost—but who are pretty sure that in the end, they'll find out who they're meant to be.

"I think it was my destiny to consider all these things I wanted to do, before I gambled on the job that was right for me. But I definitely think society gives higher status to people who say they knew what they wanted to do the second they dropped from their mother's womb."

If you're successful, Rodriguez says, it's attributed to perseverance. If not—well, that must mean you gave up. But he believes there's another factor in the mix that the world tends to gloss over: "We spend a lot of time praising people who are just lucky."

And luck, of course, can go both ways.

———————

"So much of self-help holds *us* responsible," says Wendy Simonds, a sociology professor at Georgia State University. "The idea is that we have control over our lives—*if* we follow the rules." I called Simonds because she wrote a book in 1992 titled *Women and Self-Help Culture: Reading between the Lines.* Her research interests have moved in other directions—right now she's studying the sociology of the American health care system—but she still keeps an eye on the self-improvement industry, which, in the years since her book was published, has only increased its hold on bestseller lists and its outsized influence in people's lives, teaching them that perseverance is the key to happiness.

 WHITE FLAG MOMENT

I originally wanted to be an artist. I've always loved doing art. But one day it struck me that it probably wasn't possible to make a living that way. I often wish I had found work that involved art. I've been teaching a long time—since 1985—and I think about quitting all the time now.

—*Wendy Simonds*

"Self-help makes people feel they can be experts on their own lives," she tells me. "I remember interviewing one woman for my book who had a stack of books to show me—all self-help. She felt pride that she had this motivation to self-improvement."

But even if modest personal gains are possible through a book or a podcast, they don't help the larger problems plaguing society, Simonds notes, such as systemic racism, food insecurity, and unequal access to health care. "On the whole, they're not going to solve the problems they set out to tackle, especially if they're social problems."

Those problems remain, and they grow and they fester. That could be because we're less eager to take on complicated issues such as income inequality and social injustice. It's easier to pull out a self-help book and say, *There. Right there. Did you read that? If you really give it your all, things will work out.*

To hold people responsible for their life situation, without taking into account the specifics of their struggles, and to stigmatize them for quitting, allows an unjust world to flourish. Because other people's lives are messy and complicated and essentially unknowable, and it's always so much easier just to blame.

In her 2022 novel *Mercy Street*, Jennifer Haigh includes a paragraph that channels society's blunt view of the kind of people who frequent a clinic called Wellways in a run-down Boston neighborhood: "Drug addiction and alcoholism, depression and anxiety, accidental pregnancy and sexually transmitted disease. These conditions are believed to share a common etiology, the failure of virtue. Whatever their diagnosis, all Wellways patients have this in common: their troubles are seen to be, in part or in full, their own goddamn fault."

———

So how did this happen? Did a cabal of wealthy folk gather one day in Jackson Hole or Davos and decide to make quitting the villain, as a way to keep the masses in check? (I can picture the skinny, smirking Mr. Burns from *The Simpsons*, having launched this plot against the nobodies, cackling fiendishly as he raises his copy of Smiles's *Self-Help* and waves it over his fellow zillionaires' heads as a kind of twisted benediction.)

Well, no. That's not how culture works. Culture is built by slow accretion from a variety of sources; it's a gradual accumulation of songs and stories and scholarship, of myths and gossip and advertising slogans and bumper stickers. It's not an overt process. It seeps subtly into society. It doesn't come about through legislation or executive fiat. You can't put your finger on exactly when it becomes a part of the common mindset; all you know is that one day you turn around and there it is. And it feels as if it's always been there. As Louis Menand writes in *The Free World: Art and Thought in the Cold War*, "Cultures get transformed not deliberately or programmatically but by the unpredictable effects of social, political, and technological change, and by random acts of cross-pollination."

We live in a world indoctrinated with Smiles's idea that unstinting effort will always bring rewards—and thus, by extension, if you don't get those rewards, it's your own doing. As Sarah Kendzior notes in her fiercely luminous essay collection about the American caste system and social justice, *The View from Flyover Country: Dispatches from the Forgotten America*, "When wealth is passed off as merit, bad luck is seen as bad character." You pushed the snooze button one too many times. You hopped off the treadmill too soon. You didn't believe in yourself. You gave up. And if you dare to cite other possible factors that influence your opportunities and your credit score, you're dismissed as a whiner. A crybaby.

The predilection against quitting is insidious not because it says that self-transformation is possible—it *is* possible, and it happens every day—but because it implies that the outcome of those efforts is always in our own hands. Social forces don't count. Political factors don't count. And if social forces and politics are irrelevant to destiny, why bother fixing the tax system to make it fairer? Why worry about affordable housing?

The people who run multilevel marketing firms take sly advantage of our willingness to see success and failure solely as the results of individual effort. These schemes exploit our insecurities, our vulnerabilities. We all yearn for validation—almost as much as we yearn for that extra income—and so we let ourselves be persuaded that the only way we fail is if we don't work hard enough. Falling short of sales goals can't possibly be an indictment of the products or the sales technique; it must mean we gave up too easily. Right? It's the same old culprit, in MLM as in other realms: quitting.

But quitting isn't the problem. It's the solution.

And there's a way to do it better.

PERMISSION SLIP

You keep yourself informed about the world's problems, from war and poverty to hunger and homelessness. You're starting to question the message we've been given for so many years—that if marginalized people only tried harder, they'd do fine. The myth of perseverance is often used by the powerful to demonize people in need. It's time to stop blaming—because we're all in this together.

PART III

GIVING UP: A HOW-TO GUIDE

Take a step back in order to leap higher.

—*Dudley Carleton (1573–1632)*

Chapter Seven

The Quasi-Quit: A Pause and a Pivot

We will retreat so we can attack.

—Chuck Rhoades (Paul Giamatti)
in the Showtime TV series Billions

Tiger Woods is a quitter.

Now, before you golf fans take a whack at me with a nine iron, let me explain: The man who has won fifteen major tournaments and defined excellence in a fabulously difficult sport, the man whose mantra has been "Never give up," the consummate winner, the great champion who has battled through physical and emotional distress, was never more of a champion, and never a greater competitor, than in the 2021 Masters Tournament.

He didn't triumph. He didn't come close to winning. In fact, he came in forty-seventh.

Yet for the first time, many Woods watchers noted, he seemed satisfied with not finishing first. Because he finished—period. And after suffering devastating injuries in a car accident on February 23, 2021, getting to the end of the tournament was itself a major achievement. A journalist asked, "Was this the equivalent of a victory to you, just showing up and being able to compete like you did?"

Woods's reply: "Yes."

He didn't quit the tournament. But he did quit the perfectionism that had haunted him in the past, a mindset that made anything short of absolute victory indistinguishable from crushing defeat. He stopped thinking about his work in a single, narrow way.

Like other people we'll meet in short order—some of them well-known historical figures—Woods didn't change everything about his life and his work, turning his back on all that had gone before, in a quick, definitive act. He didn't suddenly abandon the sport that has showered him with wealth and fame, or give the cold shoulder to the career that has brought his fans such pleasure as they watched him excel, time and time again. He didn't suddenly ratchet back his famously high standards for athletic performance. He wanted to win—just as fiercely as he's wanted to win for all the years he has played.

But still, he quit. He quit one way of competing—a way that required him to see only a top finish as acceptable—for another way, a way that takes the whole person and the present reality into account, a way that involves context and history.

What Woods pulled off that day was a quasi-quit. Think of it as precision quitting. It's one of several creative strategies we'll consider, a constructive way to turn that historically reviled activity—giving up—into an approach to life that just might bring you joy and satisfaction instead of frustration and shame.

This isn't quiet quitting, the trend that emerged in the fall of 2022 and involved "doing the least amount of work, just this side of being fired." Quasi-quitting isn't about slacking off and trying to slide by, hoping that no one in charge notices. It's about doing more, not less. Quasi-quitting is active, not passive. It's powered by nimbleness and acumen, not apathy.

Woods made a realistic appraisal of his current circumstances and altered his methods to fit them. In his mind, he surely shifted a few elements here, shifted some others over there. Gauged the wind direction. Leaned one way, and then the other way, assessing this moment in time just as he might calculate the best approach to a difficult putt, seeing it from a dozen different angles before selecting his club and taking his shot. From this new perspective, he was the biggest winner of all.

Bryony Harris, a woman who changed her life at age sixty-four, made a similar quasi-quit. A decade ago, after a varied career in Great Britain—she's been, among other things, an architect and a photographer—she moved to Norway and became a psychotherapist. Her chronic quits and restarts weren't really all that dramatic, she says, despite how they looked from the outside. They were matters of gradation and degree. "I have never made a decision such as 'I'm going to stop doing that and do something else,'" she told a reporter in 2022. "It's always been a gentle progression."

What Woods knows, what Harris knows, is this:

Quitting can be a rheostat dial, not just an on-off switch.

———

Leidy Klotz understands the quasi-quit. A professor of engineering, architecture, and business at the University of Virginia, he's the author of *Subtract: The Untapped Science of Less*.

"You have to fight this binary thinking," he tells me. "If you quit, it doesn't mean you can't also stick with something."

Quitting and not quitting, he adds, "are not in opposition. They're different ways to react, to make something better. There can be subtracting in the service of adding—and quitting in the service of not quitting."

Yet there's often an all-or-nothing aspect to our view of quitting, Klotz agrees. It's egged on by the notion that quitting is failing, that quitting means locking yourself into place at one end of a spectrum, instead of moving up and down the continuum as circumstances warrant. This view insists that if you quit, you lose. That quitting must be one moment in time—and a dramatic one, to boot.

Of course, quitting *can* be a flamboyant, all-or-nothing gesture. It *can* be a thunderous renunciation. It *can* involve the throwing of objects and the spewing of curses.

But quitting doesn't *have* to be any of those things. It can be thoughtful and deliberate and meditative. It can be subtle, a thing of nuance and delicacy. It can be the result of a slow-dawning realization and a gradual shift, a graceful accommodation and a canny pivot, just as it was for Charles Darwin.

On a certain spring morning in 1858, Darwin was forty-nine years old. He was at the height of his intellectual powers. He was prone to indigestion, but otherwise sound of limb. After a long sea voyage in his youth, he'd settled down in his big comfortable house with a family he cherished, there to mull over and fuss with his ideas. He was trying to figure out why so many different species crawled and flew and bounced and ran and ambled across the planet.

He was fairly certain that he'd come up with a plausible theory. There had been no *Eureka!* moment, just a series of small revelations pointing toward an interesting conclusion. But he had yet to publish his ideas. Always one more experiment was left to be performed, one more essay by a colleague to be consulted, one more fact to nail down. He was an unrepentant procrastinator, an unapologetic ditherer.

Then came word—we'll go over the particulars shortly—that somebody else had come up with a very similar idea and was poised to publish an essay about it.

This was a disaster. It meant that Darwin's entire life's work would be in vain, at least when it came to getting credit for his paradigm-shattering ideas. He'd receive little recognition for having revolutionized biology because someone else had done it first.

WHITE FLAG MOMENT

I was in my boss's office and getting chewed out. Over her shoulder I could see downtown Chicago—this tiny little skyline. I remember thinking, "That's the last time I'll be seeing that view out that window." I just knew. So when people ask me, "How do you know it's time to make the leap and quit?" I'm honest with them. I don't say, "You can do it, too." Because I have a safety net. My husband has a good job and I have health insurance through him. I talk about deciding to make what they want to do a priority—even if they can't quit their job right then. You don't have to wait for the quitting moment. Maybe that's several years out. There are so many things you can do before that.

—*Lori Rader-Day*

At that point, he had a choice. He could fume, wring his hands, curse the God he didn't believe in, and continue working as he'd always worked, doing exactly as he'd done before—plodding along, frittering away more decades in indecision and delay. He could grit his teeth and stay the course.

Or he could quit.

This wasn't a mic-drop moment. Darwin didn't smash his slides against the fireplace mantel or claw at the wainscoting. He didn't renounce his studies of the natural world. He didn't burn his manuscripts.

He gave up—but it's *how* he gave up that matters. He quit on his own terms. He quit in what today we'd call the marketing phase of his work. He began to change how he presented himself to the world. And it worked. A little over a year later, *On the Origin of Species* was published.

Quitting doesn't have to be a matter of extremes: yes or no, present or gone, now or never. It doesn't necessarily mean blowing up everything, clearing the deck, making a clean sweep. It also can mean a slight but crucial recalibration of strategies. Such a change can be just as solid and consequential as a dead stop. It's a way of taking what you already know and using it as you move forward, instead of starting from absolute zero.

That's how Dave Allen has run his life. He's always been able to parlay a passionate interest in one thing into a passionate interest in another. Quitting is a beginning for him, he says, not an end. Nothing he's learned has ever been wasted.

"It's tough being me," he informs me with a rueful laugh. "Because I have to know everything about everything!"

Born and raised in Sewickley, Pennsylvania, Allen now lives in the Cincinnati area. And he recalls with relish that special moment at fifteen when he first heard accordion music. A few lessons later, he was playing the accordion in a dance band and earning good money. He worked his way through college as a DJ at a local radio station. His romance with radio continued for more than a decade, but then gave way to his keen interest in computers.

"I took my love of computer programming and started my own custom software business," he says. He sold his products—among them, programs to measure audiences and their preferences—to radio stations. Then his attention was caught by another business: real estate. He earned his real estate license so that he could buy homes to refurbish. "A lot of people see the pivots I've made and say, 'What motivates you?' I tell them, 'Fear!'" He laughs. "I mean, what the hell am I gonna *do*?"

He means economic fear, yes. Paying bills and all the rest of it. But there's something else he fears even more: Boredom. Rust.

Getting stale. "I think that quality has kept me moving forward and reinventing myself."

In 2009 he began taking flying lessons. "I quit three times. Hardest thing I've ever done. But I always went back." He earned his pilot's license two years ago.

His wife, Karen, is a culinary arts teacher at community centers. "Sometimes she'll see me struggling with something and she'll say, 'Dave, give it up.' But I'm not a quitter." Except that he is—a quasi-quitter. And he makes the most of it.

———————

In his 2021 *New York Times* story about Vinny Marciano, a top swimmer who made a surprising swerve in his life in 2017, David W. Chen comes up with a marvelous metaphor to describe a quasi-quit. Elite athletes often feel the immense pressure of always needing to be great, Chen notes: "But what if they harbored a secret desire to stop, and wanted to start anew—to hit Ctrl-Alt-Delete, essentially?"

Quitting, that is, doesn't have to be a full stop. It can be a hesitation, a period of reflection, after which a new goal is pursued—maybe similar to the previous one, maybe not. A pause and a pivot.

Marciano had shattered records in the freestyle and backstroke as a high school swimmer in New Jersey, earning comparisons to Michael Phelps. His potential seemed limitless. But then, Chen writes, he just seemed to vanish.

He was still there. He just wasn't in the pool. Burned-out on swimming, Marciano had become a climber. His passion for athletics was unabated; he had simply redirected it. His swimming career had started to feel more like a burden than a joy, he tells Chen: "I saw a never-ending ladder—no matter what I did, there was always going to be something I was expected to achieve." Climbing provided the same physical release without the anxiety.

For non-elite athletes, it might be the opposite problem: How do you quit something at which you're mediocre at best but that you don't want to renounce completely?

In the first page of his book *How Soccer Explains the World: An Unlikely Theory of Globalization*, Franklin Foer makes a candid admission: He's a terrible soccer player. He's so bad that even the sight of his bumbles and stumbles is unbearable to those who care about him—and, presumably, about their family reputation: "When I was a boy, my parents would turn their backs to the field to avoid watching me play."

He had to choose: Soccer or self-respect?

Well—no. He didn't have to choose, after all. Foer could have both: his love of soccer *and* his desire for accomplishment. The things he does well—thinking, researching, interviewing, and writing—could be matched up with his love of a sport that he wasn't able to master as a player: "Because I would never achieve competence in the game itself," he writes, "I could do the next best thing, to try and acquire a maven's understanding." He could quasi-quit soccer.

In his book *Range: Why Generalists Triumph in a Specialized World*, David Epstein points out that the traditional view of success—it can only come from the longtime, hyper-focused devotion to an unchanging goal—is often wrong.

"Told in retrospect by popular media," Epstein writes, "stories of innovation and self-discovery can look like orderly journeys from A to B." But that's not always the case: "Research in myriad areas suggests that mental meandering and personal experimentation are sources of power, and head starts are overrated."

You'd never know that if you read your average celebrity profile, where the theme is always *Right from the start, I knew what I had to do and I did it. I didn't look right or left, only straight ahead. And of course, I never quit.*

We're told that perseverance always pays off. That the circuitous route is a time-wasting road to nowhere. That our heroes—athletes, actors, entrepreneurs, CEOs—are born knowing exactly where they want to go and then go there, without any hesitation or second-guessing or changes. That only drowsing daydreamers would bumble their way from one activity to another.

 WHITE FLAG MOMENT

At the last minute I changed my mind and went elsewhere to study political science...No one in their right mind would argue that passion and perseverance are unimportant, or that a bad day is a cue to quit. But the idea that a change of interest, or a recalibration of focus, is an imperfection and competitive disadvantage leads to a simple, one-size-fits-all...story.

—*David Epstein*

Yet as Derek Thompson reports in an *Atlantic* essay, repeatedly tweaking your career—toying with this, dabbling in that, going off in a slightly different direction—can bring rewards later, because salary surveys of various professions "found that people who switch jobs more frequently early in their careers tend to have higher wages and incomes in their prime working years. Job-hopping might seem like the work of an uncertain dilettante, but it improves the odds that you'll find a job that combines mastery, meaning, and a good amount of money."

Indeed, this "reevaluation and rerouting" of professional life, as Arianne Cohen describes it in a *Bloomberg Businessweek* article, can be a crackerjack strategy for people who are a decade or so into their careers and find themselves feeling stale and restless. The employment experts she consulted all agree that "malaise may be a sign of mastery." You've progressed as far as possible in one spot; maybe it's time to move on. And that means making a thoughtful reassessment of who you are and what you want from your life and your career—not taking an early lunch and calling it a day.

So you don't have to indulge in a wholesale dismissal of every last hope and dream you ever had. Preferable is a series of ruminative shifts and sideways shuffles. A quasi-quit can send you off in a new direction and widen your sense of possible options for your life. It's a way of giving yourself the gift of your own personal do-over—without waiting for somebody else to decree that you're worthy of one.

In a study of career paths by the Mind, Brain, and Education program at Harvard University, Epstein writes, something unexpected emerged from the data. Researchers had anticipated fairly straightforward results: the habits and routines of successful people, regardless of their fields, would be roughly similar. To their surprise, he reports, "it turned out that virtually every person had followed what seemed like an unusual path." Which leads Epstein to offer this advice: "Approach your own personal voyage and projects like Michelangelo approached a block of marble, willing to learn and adjust as you go, and even to abandon a previous goal and change direction entirely should the need arise."

———

There was no Mind, Brain, and Education program to check with back in 1723, but seventeen-year-old Benjamin Franklin knew he had to do what felt right to him, regardless of the consequences. He had no interest in paths trodden by others. He was restless and ambitious.

He was also miffed. His older brother, James, was his boss in a

Philadelphia print shop, and young Ben felt belittled and unappreci-ated. He made up his mind to bolt, writes Walter Isaacson in *Benjamin Franklin: An American Life*. Later, Franklin would return to printing, and it would become the center of his professional life and fortune. Quitting his brother's shop was a quasi-quit, a moment that looked like a fresh direction but was, in fact, a brief interlude. He would have many such temporary pivots throughout his long and busy life, stops and starts that were really just manifestations of his propulsive curiosity.

"Franklin," Edward Gray tells me, "is the absolute exemplar of cognitive nimbleness."

Gray, who teaches American history at Florida State University, says Franklin always had a great many plates spinning in the air. His endless interest in the world and how it works sent him plung-ing into one project after another, abandoning yesterday's obsession to indulge today's. The quasi-quit was a matter of strategy for him.

 WHITE FLAG MOMENT

In high school, I wanted to be a power welder. Indus-trial mechanic. I grew up building models. I made power engines for go-karts, took things apart. Very mechanically interested as a kid.

I thought, "This is what I want to do with my life." I wanted to make and break things.

But this was the late '70s. The recession. I saw a lot of despair. My parents discovered I was taking trade classes and they were freaked out. They were college educated.

I went to the University of Chicago and realized that I liked scholarly work. It was still making things.

—*Edward Gray*

Too many of his contemporary students, Gray says, don't seem to understand "polymath figures" like Franklin. It's almost as if they fear that a Franklin-style quasi-quit will signal a lack of seriousness about their careers, he adds, and slow them down. "They view it as a quaint residue of a bygone era. They're very programmed to be very single-minded and career-oriented. They have their eyes on law school or some other professional school. Most of them think they're supposed to be linear in their life course." They're missing out, he says, on the benefits of the creative meander, the rewarding roundabout, the definitely *non*linear strategy known as the quasi-quit—which can be an advantage, as we'll see, in the worlds of both business and art.

By 1996, the California-based juice company that Greg Steltenpohl had founded as a lark with his friends a half dozen years before was a monster hit. The company was racking up annual sales of almost $60 million. And then came a catastrophe: Odwalla apple juice contaminated with *E. coli* was implicated in the severe illness of dozens of people and one death. Two years later, Steltenpohl resigned from the reeling company and reassessed his life's course.

Beverages, you'd assume, would be the very last business in which he'd want to make his comeback. And yet, as the *New York Times* noted in its obituary for Steltenpohl, who died in 2021, that's exactly what he did. He started a company called Califia that sells nondairy beverages such as coffee with oat milk. What freed him to do that, his son, Eli Steltenpohl, told the *Times*, was advice given to him by Apple founder Steve Jobs, himself a legendary quasi-quitter: "Steve encouraged him to think outside the box and to look at the moment as one of opportunity for innovation and progressive thinking and not as a defeat." This is not just another iteration of the old when-life-gives-you-lemons-make-lemonade mantra. This is the audacity to quit and then resume—using some of the same gifts that got you into trouble in the first place, but with the addition of wisdom and perspective.

Creating a second company in the same product line, as Greg Steltenpohl did, required the entrepreneur to quasi-quit the hopes he'd harbored for the original business—which is similar to what Henry James did roughly a century before, with books instead of beverages.

By 1895 James had published notable novels such as *Daisy Miller* and *The Portrait of a Lady*, but he nursed a fervent desire to be a playwright. So on January 5 of that year, a jubilant James made his way through the thronged streets of London to the St. James Theatre for the opening night of his play *Guy Domville*.

The turgid drama wasn't what you'd call a crowd-pleaser. There were lots of long, windy speeches filled with ostentatiously exalted language. Audience members fidgeted. Mutters of disgust rippled through the packed house. At the end of a long address toward the play's big finish, the title character proclaimed, "I'm the last, my lord, of the Domvilles!" That caused a bored audience member to call out, "It's a bloody good thing y'are!"

Yet James's greatest humiliation was still to come. Climbing onto the stage to join the cast for the curtain call, he was greeted with "jeers, hisses, catcalls," wrote Leon Edel in *Henry James*. The actor in the title role attempted to save the day by addressing the crowd: "I can only say that we have done our very best." To which a rowdy patron yelled back, " 'Tain't your fault, guv'nor, it's a rotten play." A devastated James later confided in a letter to a friend that the opening night constituted "the most horrible hours of my life."

At that point, James could have continued to crank out plays, determined not to look like a quitter, changing his writing style and compromising his vision as he tried desperately to please the public. Or he could've gone headlong in the opposite direction, putting down his pen for keeps. He could have closed and latched the shutters on his imagination, never again risking public reaction to his work. To suddenly cease his life's calling was a drastic solution—but he had to make *some* kind of change. Another night like the one at the St. James Theatre would destroy him.

Perhaps, though, the change could be a smaller, more targeted one: a quasi-quit. So James gave up playwriting—but not writing. His chief focus returned to fiction, and he created many of the stories and novels for which he's best known today, such as *The Turn of the Screw* and *The Golden Bowl*. He would write a few more plays before his death in 1916, but for none of them did he seek the kind of large-scale production that had brought him the searing shame of *Guy Domville*.

Here's Charles Darwin on that spring morning in 1858, having just opened a letter. At this point, he's fast approaching his moment of truth. It's mere seconds away.

He's spent more than two decades—really, his entire life if you count his passionate dabbling in the study of every creature he's come across since he was a boy—silently watching and patiently thinking.

Perhaps a bit *too* patiently.

Because ever since his return two decades ago from that journey abroad to collect specimens, Darwin has gotten a bit…well, *stuck*. He spends most of his time in this grand old house in the village of Downe, some thirty-three miles southeast of London, puttering around in the laboratory he's set up exactly as he wants it, held captive by his perfectionism.

Inherited wealth means he can provide for his large family and pursue his scientific research, too, without the pesky nuisance of a day job. He's created his own private bubble of exploration and discovery. He keeps rigorous notes, but he feels no special urgency to publish them. He has the funds to do as he pleases in his own good time.

As he blithely opens a missive from a man he knows only slightly, but whom he's always respected as a fellow naturalist, Darwin has no inkling of the cataclysm to come. He scans the contents and—*poof!*—all at once his hopes, his ambitions, his dreams of renown vanish like a barnacle beneath a steep wave.

The sender is Alfred Russel Wallace, a sort of Darwinian doppelganger—minus the wealth and leisure time to sit around and think about beetles and jellyfish. From his fieldwork conducted in, most recently, Indonesia and Malaysia, Wallace has crafted an essay. He has sent it to Darwin in hopes, the accompanying letter says, that the better-connected Darwin might help him get it published.

Wallace's essay outlines a theory about how species branch into different forms. About how the struggle for survival means that some species become extinct while others flourish. It is, in short, a synthesis of the very theory upon which Darwin has been working but which he'd not yet put out into the world.

The two men have arrived at roughly the same revolutionary idea at roughly the same moment. But Wallace has written it down and actively seeks publication. And now that Darwin has read it, he can't claim to be ignorant of Wallace's work.

"It is miserable in me to care at all about priority," a distraught Darwin later will moan to friends in melancholy missives. "So all my originality, whatever it may amount to, will be smashed...I am quite prostrated & can do nothing."

At this point Darwin has a choice. He can double down on the casual attitude toward getting his work out in the world that has led him to a bad spot. He can refuse to change direction. He can stick with his routine. He can exhibit grit—and get nowhere.

Or he can quasi-quit.

He can say to himself, "Okay, so this didn't pan out as I'd hoped it would. I've got to do a few things—not *everything*, but *some* things—differently." He can reassess. Acknowledge where he went wrong.

And so he changes the way he packages and promotes his ideas, determined to set them in front of readers. After he gives up his "rights to his life's work" in his disappointed mind, as Darwin biographer Janet Browne puts it, he's able to see the task in a new light, realizing there might be a route to success, after all. Being rattled to his core has shaken him—and it has energized him, too.

This is how Browne describes it: "For so long, Darwin had been hemmed in by anxieties, always circumspect, outwardly conventional, and striving for scientific completeness...Now every impediment was pushed aside. Whereas the process of being forestalled might have destroyed a lesser spirit, Darwin emerged resolute. Steel glinted."

Gone is the diffident, hesitant man who can't stop tinkering with his theory. "Always a hard worker," Browne writes, "he worked harder than he had ever done before. Wallace's essay gave him the edge he needed." Darwin's an honorable man, and so he does help Wallace get his work published. But he also gets his own work out there, too, finally publishing *On the Origin of Species*. The quasi-quit—quitting the manner of presenting his idea, not the idea itself—enables Darwin to complete the book that Browne says is not just a scientific treatise but "a lasting work of art."

PERMISSION SLIP

You're restless. You want to try something new. You're still in the sitting-up-in-bed-in-the-middle-of-the-night-journaling-on-your-laptop stage, but it's time for a change. You're hesitant, though, to make a complete break. Why not let *some* things go—without letting *everything* go? Quitting doesn't have to be an absolute.

Chapter Eight

Quitting Your Way to Success on the Job

Strategic quitting is the secret of successful
organizations.

—Seth Godin

Suppose that on some sun-glazed, achingly beautiful day in Palo
Alto, California, in late 2014, a day with tiny clouds dotting the
blue sky like swirled dollops of whipped cream, things had gone...
otherwise.

Suppose that Elizabeth Holmes, moving with her typically brisk,
preoccupied, don't-mess-with-me stride, had walked into the headquarters of Theranos, the medical tech company she founded in
2003, and instead of immediately vanishing into her office with
barely a nod to her staff—her usual routine—she had done...some-
thing else.

Suppose she'd called an all-hands-on-deck meeting. And suppose
she'd said to the assembled employees—and repeated a few minutes
later on a conference call to journalists who cover the tech world—
"The machine doesn't work. It just doesn't. And I don't know how
to fix it. So I'm closing the company. I quit."

But that's not what she did. Instead, she spent the next several years doubling down on her claims for her new device and its potential to change the world. By 2018, the decision to quit or to persevere was taken out of her hands. The company collapsed. Holmes and her top lieutenant faced federal charges. And her dream of a revolutionary kind of blood-testing machine able to perform hundreds of tests from a single finger stick—a gizmo she'd dubbed the Edison in honor of her favorite inventor—fizzled.

To most people, Holmes's behavior is puzzling: When it first became clear that the device was a dud, why didn't she quit? Take her licks and live to fight another day? Stop, ponder, and start a new project?

The downfall of Theranos became the business world's foremost morality tale, a cautionary parable about the perils of hubris and greed and, as her detractors see it, chicanery. But it's something else as well: exhibit A in the What-Happens-If-You-Don't-Quit-Your-Job-When-You-Should-Quit-Your-Job Hall of Fame.

Because we are all Elizabeth Holmes.

No, we don't all wear black turtlenecks or drop out of Stanford to establish companies that crash and burn. But in a larger sense, yes: we are all Elizabeth Holmes. We've all been tempted to stick too long with a losing hand.

Anybody who's ever worked at any job and hit a rough patch and had to decide whether to quit or keep going is a potential Elizabeth Holmes. Whether you're the highly compensated boss or the lowest-paid employee, whether you make computer chips or cupcakes, whether you're an electrician or a teacher or a truck driver or (God help you) a writer, whether you're a hotshot entrepreneur or a hostess at Olive Garden, whether you answer to a board of directors or to a passive-aggressive middle manager named Nadine—when you feel the need to quit a situation that's plainly not working out, you face two gigantic hurdles. They're the same ones that Holmes faced—and flinched at, which is what doomed her:

First, the fear. And second, the sunk-cost fallacy.

When you're pondering an important decision about your career, you may think you're alone in your office (or in your shower, which is where some of us do our best thinking, in between the belting of Broadway show tunes), but you're not. Fear is always in the room, too. Knowing you really ought to quit, you may find yourself fretting, hesitating, dithering, delaying, and making excuses. That doesn't mean you're a coward. You're only reflecting what you've been taught. You're channeling the dubious wisdom of Samuel Smiles. Remember him? He was Mr. Self-Help, the well-meaning but misguided Victorian gentleman who recommended a fierce, unswerving, lifelong devotion to a single goal.

If you make buggy whips, then stick with buggy whips, Smiles advised. If you break stone for a living, then you'd better *keep on* breaking stone for a living, dammit; let's not hear any nonsense about quitting the quarry to go run a dairy farm or raise chickens. Changing course is for sissies. Quitting is for losers.

Lurking behind this idea of dogged, unblinking perseverance is the fear that if you quit your present job, all may be lost. What if you make a hash of the next one? And the one after that? And how do you know when it's the right moment to give up? Quitting is a risk. Leaving a less-than-perfect job and seeking a better one requires a faith in the unknown, a belief that you *will* find that ideal job, at long last. First, though, you must acknowledge and beat back the trepidation—and trust that, from the murky muddle and messy scribble that life often is, a clear, bright path will emerge.

"This definitely wasn't like the thing that I set my mind toward and then I put together all the pieces to get there" is how MSNBC anchor and author Rachel Maddow described her career trajectory to an interviewer. "I had much more of a drunken stumble through my career than you might expect...but now that I have landed here, I value it."

I can hear you murmuring, *Um, I'm not a brilliant, super-articulate person with the chops to make millions of dollars a year by hosting my own cable news show.* Just as you murmured earlier when Holmes's career was under discussion: *Um, I'm not a charismatic visionary with myriad contacts in the world of Silicon Valley venture capital.* True. You're not. And neither am I. But when it comes to the fear of quitting, we're all sisters and brothers under the skin. Quitting takes a leap of imagination into the scary void labeled "Might Work Out. Might Not. Gotta Try, Though."

Maddow, it should be noted, gave up her weeknight hosting gig on MSNBC in 2022, after almost a decade and a half, to focus on long-form projects and books. (She's still with the network, appearing one night a week and during election coverage.) Quitting doesn't faze her. In fact, it seems to fuel her.

Who knows what would've happened if Holmes had quit earlier, when it became clear that the Edison was fatally flawed? Or if Maddow had stuck with one of those early, not-quite-right jobs along her twisty road, instead of giving up and striking out in another direction? For both women, quitting—or not—marks a crucial moment in their lives, the flash point for their futures, over and over again. One didn't quit when she should have; for the other, quitting is her superpower.

Granted, it's not easy to trust that good things may come after quitting. We have absorbed Smiles's message well—the one that warns of dire consequences if we halt on our present course, the one that insists that perseverance is always the proper path. If we quit, we'll be blamed thereafter for anything bad that happens to us. Five words that nobody likes to hear: *You brought this on yourself.*

Fear is a given. It's a perfectly rational response to an unknown future. Quitting a job can mean a temporary loss of income as well as a loss of a sense of belonging, because our jobs become a big part of our identities. (We'll talk about the belonging part again in chapter 11.) Quitting a business means saying goodbye to a dream. Fundamentally, though, the fear that keeps us from quitting when we should isn't about money or camaraderie or status or ambition. It's about a belief in a better tomorrow—and how hard it can be to maintain that belief in the face of bad breaks and dumb screwups. The only way to beat fear is to cultivate optimism—and by that I don't mean some pie-in-the-sky, sunny-side-up silliness, but rather a sensible, forthright, earned optimism, the kind of optimism that needs quitting to ignite it.

If you don't believe me, maybe you'll believe Betsey Stevenson. A member of President Obama's Council of Economic Advisers and now a professor of public policy and economics at the University of Michigan, she had this to say on *The Ezra Klein Show* podcast in 2021, as a record number of people gave up their jobs:

"I mean, I remember in the 2008 recession, I would look at the quit data and be like, 'Come on, people. Quit your job. Because quits equal optimism...So take your time. Quit your job and find something better. Find the right thing for you."

Lucinda Hahn, an editor and writer, would concur. Because the penalty for *not* resigning—for letting fear keep you in a job that's not meeting your needs—can be higher than you realize, she warns.

––––––––––

Three years ago, Hahn was working for a publisher in North Carolina when a management shakeup left her in a vulnerable spot. "I started to get ignored. It was one thing after another. They didn't want to fire me. I was a valuable member of the team. I was being paid very well—I'd gotten a thirty percent raise and a promotion the year before." But she was bored by her assignments now and her newly narrowed horizons.

"You want to say, 'Fuck you. I'm leaving.' But you don't. And when you're being treated poorly and you don't stand up for yourself, there *is* a cost."

Hahn was surprised, she tells me, that she couldn't just do what she'd always done before: resign and set about finding the right job. A capacity for cutting her losses and moving on quickly had become her go-to survival mechanism, she says, first developed after a difficult experience during her college years at Northwestern University, where she played tennis and softball. "My identity was wrapped up in the idea that I was an athlete. I kept injuring my knee over and over again. At some point, I knew I had to stop playing sports but I didn't want to—and then I injured my knee catastrophically."

 WHITE FLAG MOMENT

I'd been working in Prague about six months. A friend of mine was working at the same place. I remember when she told me she was quitting. I was like, "Nobody does that! You mean you can just do that? You can just *quit*?" I thought about it for about two weeks and then I quit, too. I was grateful to her for planting that seed. It felt like a weight lifting. Like a curtain opening. It was such a powerful moment.

—*Lucinda Hahn*

She could've avoided a lot of ligament damage, Hahn recalls, if she'd given up competitive sports earlier—but athletics was more than just a pastime. It lived at the very center of her self-image. "I grieved when I had to stop playing. I remember calling my mom and crying and saying, 'I don't have anything to offer anyone.' I needed something to fill up that hole—the one that was there when I quit playing."

After college, she'd begun to work on herself, determined to learn a different way of being in the world. She wanted to make decisions based on her own desires, not somebody else's expectations. She wanted to be judged for the kind of person she was—not on her achievements, not on her salary or job title. Along the way, she followed her heart, quitting jobs when they no longer challenged her or when the working conditions became untenable.

That's why she was flummoxed by the situation in which she found herself in North Carolina: stuck in a job that made her miserable, that no longer tapped her talents or fed her soul. She understood the benefits of strategic quitting—she'd seen it do the trick, over and over again, in her own life and the lives of friends. So why couldn't she pull it off this time?

A sudden squall of fear, she says, had caused her to forget her number one life rule: "Quitting can be incredibly liberating." Once she recognized that it was fear holding her back, she rediscovered her courage. Naming the foe helped her vanquish it. She negotiated a good severance package on her way out the door, sold her house, and moved to a small town in northern Michigan, where she quickly found an excellent remote-work position—and a life she loves.

The other factor that keeps us from quitting jobs when we should? The infamous concept known as the sunk-cost fallacy. We may not have created a company that's worth some $9 billion, as Theranos was at its peak, but we all know what it's like to cram time, money, effort, and hope into an enterprise about which we care deeply. That makes us reluctant to give up, even when it's clear that giving up is what we need to do. We keep going even when it becomes abundantly clear that we ought to stop—because we're trying to redeem the time, money, and emotional energy we've already invested. Yet the part we've put in is gone. It's irretrievable. We know we *should* quit—but quitting feels like a waste of resources as well as a defeat. So we hang on for too long, for the wrong reasons.

Holmes, like each of us, surely has private psychological peccadillos that influence her actions, and there's a risk of oversimplification when we do postmortems on cratered careers. But in broad strokes, if she'd acted more like her device's namesake, she might have embarked on another startup. And this one might have been successful. When it became obvious to insiders that Edison (the machine) didn't work, Holmes could have followed the example of Edison (the human being): Quit. Recalibrate. It's an option available to all of us, whether we're employees or entrepreneurs.

The way to sink the sunk-cost fallacy? Channel your inner Edison. Because the man was a virtuoso of quitting.

———

Trial and error—repeatedly abandoning a fruitless path to free up time, money, and moxie to find a more promising one—was his specialty. If Edison could've patented quitting as a proprietary methodology, he surely would have. He understood how valuable quitting is for ultimate success. If something doesn't work, you stop. And hunt down something that does.

Edison's uncanny flair for quitting is reflected in his long search for an American-grown plant that could produce rubber, a project that obsessed him from the years just prior to World War I until his death in 1931. The quest constituted the last big adventure of his life, according to biographer Edmund Morris. Rubber was an important commodity; it won wars and, in peacetime, could make or break economies. Many historians compare the significance of rubber in the early twentieth century to the place oil holds in the world today—it was essential, and there never seemed to be enough of it available from accessible places.

This was precisely the sort of challenge that would cause Edison to bolt from his chair, fling away a chewed-up cigar, and rush headlong to his workshop. Instead of depending on sap from trees that grew in places like South America and Southeast Asia, he dreamed of producing rubber in his own laboratories, using plants found in the United States. The odyssey required the kind of clockwork quitting that defined Edison's most important achievements.

From every plant he came across, including milkweed and dandelions and goldenrod and oleander and honeysuckle and fig trees and guayule and more than seventeen thousand others, he'd extract the sap and try to vulcanize it. "He seemed unable to drive past a weed patch without jumping out in search of milky varieties," Morris wrote. Over and over again, Edison believed he'd found the right plant. After some promising results, he'd write PHENOMENON in his notes—all caps—by the plant's name, but further experiments invariably proved disappointing. He'd give up and then go on to the next one.

If he'd stayed stuck on the potential of a single plant—the dandelion, say—and refused to budge, patting himself on the back for not being a quitter, he would have wasted time and effort. Quitting was his measure of success, not failure. To Edison, quitting was a forward march, not a backward stumble.

And even if he didn't prevail—synthetic rubber was developed by others, after his death—it was the way he went about his mission that matters. It's a template that any of us can follow. We may not be geniuses, but we can learn how to make quitting work for us.

 WHITE FLAG MOMENT

My father-in-law just got fed up with teaching. He and his wife had always loved California. So he called us and said, "I quit." We were like, "You *what*?" He said, "I've been dabbling in piano tuning. We're going to go find a place where 'Ballenger' is the first piano tuner in the Yellow Pages." They sold everything and left Iowa. All they took was one U-Haul and two dogs.

—*Cathy Ballenger*

To use the phrase made famous by Sheryl Sandberg, formerly a top executive with Facebook, Edison leaned in to quitting. He cultivated techniques for serial quitting. He understood that true perseverance is never about not quitting—it's about quitting strategically, and smartly, and with gusto and flair. It's about enduring the fits and starts, the ups and downs, that occur in any worthwhile quest.

Like business, science "isn't a straightforward progression," says Guy Dove. "Its history can be messy and sometimes catastrophic." Viewed from the pristine perch of the present, the path to scientific and technical breakthroughs can look like a smooth, easy trek going up and up and up, in which every mistake is part of the plan, every disaster just additional proof that you're heading in the right direction.

That's not how it really happens, of course—but that's how it appears after the fact.

Dove, a philosophy professor at the University of Louisville, taught a course at the Louisville Free Public Library in the spring of 2022 on how failure and quitting boost scientific progress— eventually. Meanwhile, it's not easy for anybody to live in the midst of the chaos and uncertainty of a new venture.

"In profiles of Elon Musk or Steve Jobs—or whoever we're fan-boying over at the moment—it's, 'Look at all these failures that led to success.' But we need to be very careful about that," Dove tells me. "Not so much to demystify failure, but to understand how arbitrary it is.

"There's a new model in business schools now—this idea of 'failing your way to success.' It's become a trope—seeing failure as a way of achieving success. I'm suspicious of that because it can be misleading."

When you wring your hands over questionable decisions you've made about your career, remember that at the time you made them, you didn't know what was coming. You did the best you could with the information at hand. Going forward, be sure that when you make those decisions, quitting is always on the table as an option.

"The way I look at it, we don't quit enough," declares John A. List. "Society has taught us that quitting is bad. 'Quitting' is a repugnant term. But quitting is like calling an audible in football. There are NFL quarterbacks who are glorified because they quit a bad play— and when they did that, they put their team in a better position to win."

WHITE FLAG MOMENT

By the end of that weekend...I came to terms with the fact that no matter how much I cared about golf and practiced it—and no matter what it symbolized for me—I was never going to be good enough to make it onto the PGA tour, or even come close...So I decided it was time to quit on my dream.

—*John A. List*

List, economics professor at the University of Chicago and former chief economist for Uber and Lyft, devotes a chunk of his latest book, *The Voltage Effect: How to Make Good Ideas Great and Great Ideas Scale*, to the positive aspects of quitting. In a marvelous chapter titled "Quitting Is for Winners," he argues that "getting good at quitting is one of the secrets for scaling successfully," adding that companies "must be willing to give up on an idea that is going nowhere, thereby freeing time and resources to invest in other directions where a breakthrough edge might emerge." Another name for that is opportunity cost.

Part of the problem, List tells me, is lingo: "When people hear the word 'quit,' they think, 'They're going to quit and lie in bed all day.' That's why the word 'pivot' is good. 'Pivot' is quit and then start something new. Pivoting is not only quitting, but also starting."

Whether you're an employee or the boss, the possibility of quitting needs to be considered if things start to go sideways. Otherwise, your business can end up like a Theranos or a WeWork, another company whose troubles begged the question: When problems began piling up, why didn't they just quit and try something else?

Through his charm and salesmanship, WeWork founder Adam Neumann managed to keep a bad idea going for a very long time, according to Eliot Brown and Maureen Farrell, authors of *The Cult of We: WeWork, Adam Neumann, and the Great Startup Delusion*: "He made those across the table see the future he saw...It was, at its heart, a magic trick," they wrote. And then the trick stopped working. By 2015, WeWork was losing $1 million per day. Its downfall is dramatized in the 2022 Apple TV+ series *WeCrashed*. (The Theranos debacle also showed up as a TV series, *The Dropout*, premiering the same year on Hulu. As source material for our entertainment, we can't seem to get enough of these Icaruses of the business world who plummet back down to earth with fiery flamboyance.)

Holmes and Neumann have strong egos. They care very much about how they look to other people, from their investors to their employees to the awed readers of magazine profiles. Yet a key reason for their downfall—and for the stumble of anyone who doesn't give up when it's prudent to do so—might be found in an excessive concern for how they look to themselves.

Self-image can be a significant barrier to strategic quitting, according to Adam Grant, professor at the University of Pennsylvania's Wharton School, and author of many best-selling business books. Just as it can keep a CEO from acting swiftly to head off a debacle, it can keep people locked into unfulfilling jobs in unappealing workplaces.

"I've heard this countless times from my students at Wharton," Grant tells me. "They're afraid to walk away from abusive bosses, toxic cultures, and misguided career choices due to the fear of being a quitter. It's not just the image—it's also identity. Yes, they're worried about looking like quitters, but they're also very concerned about seeing *themselves* as quitters. You don't want to look in the mirror and see a person who gives up staring back at you."

With that mindset, it's no wonder that so many of us are reluctant to quit. Quitting means we couldn't cut it on the job. We let everybody down—especially ourselves. And the world keeps reminding us that giving up is a sign of wobbly weakness. Yet we forget that quitting is a survival instinct, that our brains are good at it for a reason, and that we have the capacity to overwrite the cultural narratives that give it the misleading gloss of a moral failing. (Thanks for nothing, Samuel Smiles.) Quitting remains the nuclear option—which is a shame, because when employed strategically, when used with precision and creativity, it can restart a stalled career or propagate a new business.

When clients come to her, says Ruth Sternberg, they're commonly at a crossroads, and they're often afraid to put quitting on their list of options. A career counselor based in Rochester, New York, she specializes in helping people in midcareer find the confidence to change fields or to start their own businesses, especially because they may be doing okay—not great, but okay—right where they are. They're apprehensive about losing the seniority they've built up in an existing career.

"It's a huge struggle," she tells me. "I can sense their fear of failure. They don't say it out loud, but it's an undertone."

 WHITE FLAG MOMENT

A bunch of stuff started piling up at the paper. I thought, "If I have to go out one more time on a cold winter day and find a bunch of people sledding and interview them, I'm going to scream." So I sat down and started brainstorming. I sat in my car and pretended I had my own business and was describing it to someone else.

—*Ruth Sternberg*

She knows the feeling. Burned-out after many years of working in journalism and publishing in the Midwest, she was determined to quit and start her own business in a different field, developing a new skill set. But making a radical shift meant altering how she saw herself. And that, she recalls, was more daunting than any other aspect of her personal metamorphosis from employee to small-business owner.

We're often told that big changes are only possible if you're in your twenties or early thirties, as if there's a sell-by date on dreams. Sternberg rejects that. To people who want to quit their jobs and try something else, yet find that the idea fills them with apprehension because they're not fresh out of college, she has this advice: come up with a realistic assessment of your value to a potential employer. Your worth in the marketplace is found not only in the amount of relevant experience in a particular field, but also in an ability to forge connections in *any* field, in flexibility, in a dynamic mindset. "It's not about your resume," she declares. "It's about your relationships."

Not everyone wants to quit their day job and be an entrepreneur. But those who do are in luck, Sternberg says: "It's much more acceptable now to start your own business. I tell them to look at people who are inventing new and exciting things. People adapt. They always have. This is how the world progresses."

Yet it's not easy to transcend the truisms we've heard for years about the downside of quitting. As List writes in *The Voltage Effect: How to Make Good Ideas Great and Great Ideas Scale*, "Choosing the intense but brief pain of quitting now over the prolonged pain of failure later is a skill that both individuals and organizations must cultivate.

"You must quit," he adds, "to give yourself another chance at winning."

Jack Zimmerman can personally attest to that. He can fill you in on the surprising utility of quitting—and he'll be happy to do so if you ask, because he's a storyteller extraordinaire.

He's many other things, too. He's a musician and a photographer. He's an attentive dad and a doting grandfather and an adoring husband. He's a fancier of bicycles and opera. The one thing he's definitely *not*, however, is a businessman.

He tried to be.

He quit.

Think of Zimmerman as the anti-Holmes. He realized that he couldn't keep doing the wrong thing just because somebody might call him a quitter. True, he didn't have a fancy headquarters in Palo Alto, or a high-powered board of directors, or *Wall Street Journal* reporters sniffing around his office, asking uncomfortable questions about his balance sheet. But it was still hard at first to say, "I quit," he admits, and to not hear it in his own ears as *I'm a bum*.

"I have no regrets now about anything I've quit," declares Zimmerman, who lives in a high-rise condo in downtown Chicago with his wife, Charlene. "And there have been several things! Initially I wanted to be a trombonist in a symphony. I didn't want it as a hobby—I wanted it as a *profession*. But I wasn't equipped talent-wise to pull that off." So he let go of that ambition and was glad of it: "I'd have had a very unhappy life, going to auditions and not winning any."

Next, he tells me, he opened a piano store in a Chicago suburb, with a side hustle as a piano tuner. He tried for fifteen years to make it work—but he wasn't cut out for a business career.

It was one of the lowest points of his life. "To fail at a business—it hurts. It's like a divorce."

WHITE FLAG MOMENT

I was just so unhappy—working alone most days. I'm a social person. Being alone in a room with a piano didn't do it for me. I needed to get out. I needed to *breathe*. So I put the place up for sale.

—*Jack Zimmerman*

Fortunately, he never had to worry about a real divorce, only the metaphorical kind. His wife, now retired after a three-decade career as principal clarinet player at Chicago's Lyric Opera, "was incredibly supportive. She was brilliant."

After bowing out of his business career, he returned to his first passion: storytelling. Think David Sedaris with a Chicago accent and you'll get a sense of Zimmerman's skill as a raconteur, of his humor and his appealingly sideways view of life, as he shares his tales of Old Chicago—the world of pipe fitters and politicians on the make—in one-man shows around the city and on YouTube. He's worked as a columnist for magazines and newspapers, and in public relations for several music venues in the Chicago area.

Regrets? Nah.

"I've seen a lot of people who are really unhappy who *don't* quit," he says. "They spend their lives struggling. Me, I've been happy to get to the next step."

It's a chilly fall night in Bexley, Ohio, when I meet Lesli and Mike Mautz for the first time. But the chill doesn't stand a chance against Lesli.

Within about twenty seconds of my arrival, she has the fireplace going in the dining room, and by the time we settle in to talk, everything's warm and comfy and welcoming—which, as it happens, is precisely the sort of atmosphere you want in a bed-and-breakfast.

I've come by to ask Lesli and Mike—who joins us a few minutes later, accompanied by their pint-sized and well-behaved rescue dog, Cole—how they did it: how they quit their jobs, their comfort zones, and (said some friends at the time) their grip on sanity to sink their time, their energy, and a considerable portion of their life savings into a business about which they knew, in round numbers, approximately this: zero.

 WHITE FLAG MOMENT

Quitting Joie de Vivre...wasn't easy as it defined not just my professional identity but my personal identity as well. [He was founder of the hotel chain.] But sometimes, there needs to be divine intervention—I had a flatline experience due to being allergic to an antibiotic—or friends who help you see what you're not willing to see yourself.

—*Chip Conley*

Before they'd even opened their doors for the first time in 2013, their building costs for renovating the venerable structure were triple what they'd budgeted for. The unexpected need for all new plumbing and electrical—plus eleven thousand square feet of new drywall—blew up the initial estimates.

"Sometimes," Mike says ruefully, "it's better to go in blind."

Yet it all worked out. The Bexley Bed and Breakfast is a handsome place, a rambling brick building set amidst the quiet, tidy elegance of Bexley, a Columbus suburb known for its large old homes adorned with slate roofs and leaded windows. I'd love to be able to say, "Stop by and say hello to the Mautzes and stay the night at the B and B."

But I can't. Because by the time you read this, the Mautzes will have moved on to their next adventure. They're short-timers on this brisk autumn night.

I find them, in other words, on the cusp of yet another jump. They have recently sold the business to a small college in the area, which will continue to operate it as a B and B. Their experience provides another valuable lesson about the business of quitting:

Just as the opportunities to *start* new businesses and sign on to new jobs are everywhere, so, too, are the opportunities to quit them. And maybe start another. Or maybe not.

Not all endings are tragedies. Sometimes they're just stations along the way to somewhere else—somewhere better, or somewhere worse, because everything is perpetually changing, but this much is indisputable: somewhere different.

Quitting isn't always a decision that you make voluntarily. At times, it's thrust upon you. You quit because you have to, not because you want to. Still, there are ways of making even that contingency— giving up when you're cornered—into something positive, into a springboard for your next leap forward.

On the evening of December 9, 1914, shortly after sunset, a quantity of nitrate stock stored in a small building on the grounds of Edison's sprawling laboratory complex in New Jersey caught fire. The flames spread quickly, gobbling up thirteen buildings while he and others watched from a high point nearby.

No one was harmed in the blaze, but the damage was substantial: Destroyed were raw materials and prototypes, much of the elaborate infrastructure that had enabled America's most famous inventor to average a new invention every eleven days for forty years.

"Am pretty well burned out," Edison announced in a prepared statement to the reporters who showed up the next morning to see how he'd respond to this setback, "but tomorrow there will be some rapid mobilizing when I find out where I'm at." He would bounce back from adversity, as was his custom. And he would do what he always did, which is to use quitting as inspiration.

Edison never invented a time machine, although if he had, and if he'd used it to catapult himself into the twenty-first century, I like to think he would've gotten in touch with Holmes shortly after her device failed its initial tests—a debacle that constituted another kind of fire, slow-burning but ultimately just as ruinous.

You can imagine what the old man would've said to her: "Stop what you're doing right now, young lady, and find another way to make this machine do what you're claiming it can do. If you can't find another way, then quit. And invent something else. And in the meantime—don't put my name on it until the dad-burned thing *works*." Quitting was not failure in Edison's book; it was the first step toward success.

Standing on the hill that night, surrounded by anxious colleagues and stunned family members, watching the flames leap and glow, Edison was approached by a devastated employee who termed the fire, in a trembling voice, "an awful catastrophe."

The staffer didn't understand his boss at all. The charm and challenge of life was what you did *after* you were forced to quit. You made plans to scratch through the smoldering ruins for something—anything—upon which you might build again. And in the meantime, you enjoyed the spectacle.

Edison's cheerful response to his gloomy underling: "Yes,

Maxwell, a big fortune has gone up in flames tonight, but isn't it a beautiful sight?"

PERMISSION SLIP

You're discouraged. You're frustrated. The job's not working out as you'd hoped it would. Or maybe you started your own business and it failed. Time to channel your inner Edison. Don't fall victim to fear—or to the sunk-cost fallacy or to failing to heed opportunity cost. Quitting isn't the end. It can be the beginning of success.

Chapter Nine

Quitter's Guilt: What If I Disappoint the People I Love?

I hope you live a life you're proud of, and if you find
that you're not, I hope you have the strength to
start all over again.

—*Eric Roth*

Stephany Rose Spaulding had put it off as long as possible. But it was crunch time. She had to tell her dad she'd decided to quit.

They were sitting in his car in a parking lot, she recalls, after running an errand together. Spaulding was visiting her parents on Chicago's South Side. She'd driven there from Lafayette, Indiana, where she was a doctoral candidate in the American studies program at Purdue University.

"Nobody in my family had ever earned a PhD," Spaulding tells me, explaining why the stakes felt so high at that moment. Her mother and father, both public school teachers, had been thrilled when she'd entered grad school, proud of their daughter with her scholarships and her ambitions.

But there was a problem they didn't know about, because she'd never revealed it to them. She hadn't wanted them to worry about her. Now, though, four years in, she had reached a crisis point. She was miserable. One of the few Black students in her department, she felt marginalized and disrespected. And definitely out of place.

"It was such a strain," she recalls. "Just the level of racism. West Lafayette was one of the most toxic places I've ever lived in. It was weighing on me."

She'd decided to quit the program. How, though, could she break the news to her parents—especially her father, who believed that the Almighty had destined her for an academic career?

You move through multiple worlds. You're the child of your parents, and if you have children yourself, you're a parent, too. You may be surrounded as well by siblings, a partner, close friends, neighbors, extended family members, plus bosses and colleagues. Having people care about you, and harbor high expectations for you, is wonderful. Those expectations can guide you, inspire you, and pick you up when you falter.

But when you face a decision about quitting—a job, school, a relationship—those bonds mean that you must take into account more than just your own view. If other people don't believe it's a good idea for you, the same benevolent forces that keep you going can work the opposite way: they can exert an extra pressure that may run counter to your sense of what's right for you. Because none of us wants to disappoint the people we love, the people who know us best (or think they do), the people whose dreams for us have been a guiding star throughout our lives.

When Spaulding told her father in the car that day that she'd decided to leave Purdue, he was upset, she recalls: "He started yelling at me. 'God sent you there! Are you going to walk away from God?'"

She told him what she'd been going through: "Almost every day, I was suicidal. I'd witnessed other Black grad students have nervous breakdowns. One of my good friends—it got so bad for her that she couldn't hold her hand steady to drink a cup of coffee."

Her father settled down and listened to her. He apologized for sounding harsh. And she listened to him, too. He suggested that maybe she could find a way to make it work. He offered to brainstorm strategies with her. They'd pray about it together.

"I was experiencing such tension," she remembers. "Do you stick with it? Or change what you need to do to get to the next level of your life?"

 WHITE FLAG MOMENT

I was devastated. My dissertation committee had just rejected my second proposal…I sat down with one of my committee members in his apartment. He was one of my favorite professors. I said, "I don't know how I'm going to finish this degree." He said, "You've done the work, Stephany. The dissertation is just an exercise. Do the damned exercise."

I remember his apartment was dark. The sun was setting outside. I was like, "I'm sitting here in the dark." He was like, "Just do what the white people want you to do." I'd have to find a way to do that but still survive! I knew in that moment I was going to leave Lafayette.

—*Stephany Rose Spaulding*

From the time she was a child, she'd given a great deal of thought to how she wanted to use her gifts. "Growing up, I always thought

I'd be a lawyer," Spaulding tells me, adding with a laugh, "I was enamored with Clair Huxtable from *The Cosby Show*. I thought I'd go back east, live in a brownstone, have this middle-class life where poets and musicians would be in and out of my kids' lives." After her sophomore year in college, one of her professors approached her and asked if she'd ever thought of an academic career. "It was so disruptive to my thinking," she recounts. "I was like, 'That's not what Black people *do*.'

"Then she said, 'You have a knack for this. And they'll pay you to go.' I said, 'You should've led with that!'" But grad school wasn't the dream scenario she'd envisioned. Her doubts accumulated, until finally there she was, sitting in a car with her dad, anguished and uncertain. She knew what her parents wanted her to do—but what did *she* want? Should she quit, which struck her as the best course under the circumstances—or try to push through, with her family's blessing?

Spaulding remained in the PhD program but she moved from West Lafayette. She rented an apartment in Chicago and wrote her dissertation there, driving back to campus when necessary but mostly sticking around her new home, relishing her life in a bigger, more diverse city.

"My advisors were horrified," she recalls. "They were sure I'd never finish my dissertation in absentia." But they didn't know her and her determination.

She polished off her dissertation, graduated, and after several teaching jobs, she became the interim chancellor for diversity, equity, and inclusion at the University of Colorado at Colorado Springs, while also teaching in the university's department of women's and ethnic studies.

She'll never forget the day she sat in that parking lot next to her father, trying to decide what was right for her life. She had to make the decision by herself—but no matter how things worked out, she knew she'd never truly be alone.

———————

In few places are judgments about quitting as stark and unequivocal as they are in the world of sports. If you drop out, you're a wimp; if you keep fighting, you're a winner. To many people, in fact, the word "quitter" automatically conjures up an image of someone trudging off a dusty field in defeat, helmet doffed, shoulders slumped. Or just not showing up for the next practice. Quitting seems about as straightforward a proposition as the final score on a scoreboard.

Not so fast, says Dr. Kristen Dieffenbach.

"There's a difference between choosing to stop and *quitting*," she tells me. "That word has a lot of vitriol to it. We equate quitting with failure. That's not necessarily the case. There can be times when you stop doing something because it's dangerous and unhealthy. But we put such a high value on outcomes in sports, and if you quit, it's because you 'couldn't hack it.'"

Dieffenbach is the director of the Center for Applied Coaching and Sport Sciences, as well as an associate professor of athletic coaching education at West Virginia University. She's an athlete herself, as is her husband, and they're the parents of a young athlete. In other words, she's got a lot of skin in the quitting-or-not-quitting game.

A prime focus of Dieffenbach's research and teaching is the role that authority figures like parents and coaches play in the lives of young athletes. These relationships complicate the idea of quitting, she points out, because there's more involved than just one person's decision to give up. Substantial investments of money and time and emotional energy have gone into helping the athlete develop their skills. We never quit anything on our own—or just for ourselves. Quitting is never a solo sport.

WHITE FLAG MOMENT

I was working on a story in the newsroom. On deadline. My son Ryan was nine years old then, and I was coach of his Little League team. I remember looking up at the clock, hoping I'd finish that story on time. It was the first time in my life I wanted to be somewhere other than a newsroom. That was it. I had to find something else to do so I could be at those games. I believe that half of parenting is just showing up—and I wanted to show up. That's when I knew I had to quit.

—*Robin Yocum*

"Sports can be a very emotional arena for a family," Dieffenbach tells me. "For parents, there can be a lot of driving, a lot of sitting in the stands. So when a child quits a sport, it's not just the child quitting—it's the whole family."

For parents and coaches, accepting a young athlete's decision to abandon a sport is a tough ask. There's a transactional aspect to the mentoring that often comes with organized sports: *I did this for you, I sacrificed, I believed in you—and now you're quitting? Just when it's all starting to pay off?*

If a coach pushes someone past their comfort level, are they a motivator—or a monster? The tales of tough coaches who demand excellence from their players, and who won't allow them to quit, are the rough stuff of legend. We celebrate professional mentors such as Vince Lombardi, the Green Bay Packers coach who was known for pushing players to their breaking points, and current New England Patriots coach Bill Belichick, similarly lauded as a leader who drives his players mercilessly—and who gets great performances out of them.

Bobby Knight, hard-charging head coach of the Indiana University men's basketball team from 1971 to 2000, was routinely celebrated despite multiple public tantrums unleashed upon his team and at least one documented case of physical abuse against a player during practice. A few quit—but most revere him and credit him with their success.

But don't people always have the option to leave? The players who had an issue with Knight's temper could've walked away. They could've said no. It wasn't a gulag.

In a technical sense, that's true. The gym doors weren't locked. In a practical sense, however, they were trapped—not by sealed doors but by expectations and imagery. The title character in the film *Rocky*, battered and bloody but unbowed, fights to the end. The psychological cost of quitting can cancel out any thoughts of stopping. Heroes hang in. They don't fold.

"There's definitely a shame associated with quitting," Dieffenbach says. "In my twenty-five-year career as a runner, I've quit a race twice. And I'm still incredibly ashamed of that."

Shame is a powerful motivator—not only the shame that we may internalize if we give up, but also the shame we feel if we think we've disappointed those who believe in us, like parents and coaches. To avoid it, we may ignore signals from our bodies that it's time for a break. "Some athletes don't know the difference between 'This is pain that I should push past' and 'This is pain I need to pay attention to,'" Dieffenbach says. Which means it's not as simple as just declaring flatly, "Okay, so everybody should stop when they come across an impediment." We know that's not helpful, either. There's real value in persevering in physical endeavors, just as there is in intellectual ones when you're learning a new subject and you hit a rough spot. "You do have to push through the pain and keep going," Dieffenbach says. "Our brains say, 'You need to turn back.' Anyone who's gone to a gym after a few months of inactivity knows the truth of that. But that doesn't mean we should always listen."

The choice between, on one hand, keeping at it and experiencing the joy of doing something that surpasses what you thought were your limits and, on the other hand, quitting is sometimes a hard one to make. "We have a history of valuing hard work, and quitting is seen as failure. The narrative is, 'Oh, you quit'—not, 'Oh, you chose to do something else with your time.' Quitting is analogous to failing."

 WHITE FLAG MOMENT

My husband and I and our five-year-old son, Michael, decided to travel. Everyone thought I was making a horrible mistake [by quitting her job]. The number of people who said, "You can't quit—you're sabotaging your career!" was staggering. But we thought, "Why not?" My mother drove us to the airport, and when we got there, she turned to me and said, "I'll probably die while you're on a kibbutz in Israel." But somehow I found the gumption to leave. Everyone told me I'd regret it. I never did.

—*Bonnie Miller Rubin*

Dieffenbach can't remember a time in her life when she wasn't running. Or cycling. Or playing tennis. Or—well, name your sport, and she's probably participated in it, giving it all she's got. She loves competition, loves grinding out a win, loves testing herself against other people. But even better than that, she says, is testing herself today against who she was yesterday.

She was a walk-on for the Boston University track team. When she started her graduate work in physical education, her interest expanded from the simple physiology of sports—what happens to our bodies when we run and jump and swing a bat or a hockey stick?—outward into the world itself. She wanted to apply the lessons she'd learned as an athlete to other human endeavors.

"'How do we support human potential and growth through sport? Can I help change the culture?' That's what I asked myself."

Dieffenbach wishes that America's love of sports was less about watching elite athletes playing in professional leagues like the NBA and the NFL and more about... the rest of us, playing in our backyards. Keeping active and fit because it's fun and it feels good—not because we're aiming at a pro career. That way, the Quitting Moment might never have to come in the first place, because we never get fed up or become trapped by perfectionism. We're having fun.

"We have such a solo entrepreneurial mindset in the United States," she says. "Other countries have a communal mindset. We have a bad habit of thinking of sports as only valuable if you're 'going for the gold.' We don't do a good job of recognizing sports as a lifetime engagement with the sport itself."

Dieffenbach and her husband are both "driven athletes," she reports. Their home has three dogs, two cats—and fifteen bikes in the basement. Their eleven-year-old son plays hockey.

What if she came home one day and he announced he was quitting?

"I'd say, 'That's okay. But what else are we going to do to stay physically active? You're not going to sit home and watch YouTube videos.' I wouldn't be upset at all. But I'd have the conversation about why."

Heidi Stevens doesn't have to wonder what she'd say if her seventeen-year-old daughter June decided to quit gymnastics, a sport June started at age six. Because that's just what happened last year. Her daughter got in the car one day after practice and said, "I'm done. Is that okay?"

"I was like, 'Hell, yes!'" Stevens admits with a laugh. "We'd been driving thirty minutes each way, four nights a week, to get to the gym. When she said she wanted to quit, I was thrilled."

But her daughter's bulletin was the beginning, not the end, of the topic, Stevens goes on to say. "Parenting culture has changed now. We're more involved in our kids' social and emotional lives. With my own kids, we talk things through. Take things on a case-by-case basis. No hard rules."

Stevens writes a syndicated column about parenting issues and is creative director of the University of Chicago's Parent Nation, which advocates for family issues such as affordable child care and better health care options. She used her own quitting history, she says, as a template for how she *didn't* want to raise June and June's younger brother, Will.

"In high school I was pretty directionless. Gymnastics, ballet, tap—I did those things and then gave them up. I played piano from first grade to high school. But when I was playing, my brother would come along and hit me and then my mother would yell at him. So there was always a lot of tension. And it wasn't just that—I hated practicing."

Which is why she talked it over with her daughter when the Quitting Moment came along.

"It's hard to stick it out," Stevens says. "I told her if she wanted to quit, it couldn't be just because it's hard and not fun."

She doesn't want her daughter to have any regrets. Because there's a wistfulness in Stevens's voice when she adds, "I wish I had stuck with piano. I could have been very good."

Interviewed separately, June Stevens backs up her mother's account. "She was supportive when I did gymnastics, but she was also, 'You don't have to do this.'"

 ## WHITE FLAG MOMENT

I remember it vividly. I had just gotten done with gymnastics practice. I walked out of the gym and I saw my mom's car—it was a silver Honda CR-V—there in the parking lot, where she always waited for me. I just thought, "Okay, I'm done. I'm never coming back here." It was scary, being done with something you've done most of your life—but it was also a good feeling. It felt like I was in control. I turned around and took a picture of the gym and then I got in the car and said, "Mom, this is goodbye."

—*June Stevens*

Her decision to quit was the culmination of several factors, she says. She'd started at a new gym after many years with a favorite coach at a different gym, a coach who'd left the area. The new gym didn't feel the same. But how could it? The old gym "was my family," she recalls. "I have a lot of good memories."

Her decision to quit came quickly. And just as fast, she joined her school's rowing team and then the cheer squad. She gave up crew—"It was boring"—but has stuck with cheer. She doesn't much care what sport she's playing. What matters is staying in motion: "I like the feeling of everything being sore. The pure athletic part of it."

Lewis Hanes couldn't ask his father for advice, couldn't check with the old man to see if it was a smart move or a dumb one to quit the job, if it would serve him well or be something that, years later, he'd shake his head over.

His father had died of an infection in 1938 when Hanes was six years old, leaving his mother to run the family's soybean farm in northwestern Ohio and raise him and his three sisters. And maybe it was that fact—the absent presence of his father—that helped push him. An authority figure can influence us even if they're not physically present anymore. A decision to quit or to stay can be the result of invisible forces.

Many people still hear a grandparent's or a parent's voice in their heads, offering commentary on a crucial choice. Nobody else can hear it. But that doesn't matter. The decision can still feel like a collaboration.

Hanes was eighteen years old, fresh out of high school, class of 1950. He took a job at the Perry-Fay Manufacturing plant in Elyria, Ohio, picking that job over other offers because "a neighbor drove there every day and I didn't have a car."

Eight hours a day, every day, he inspected the screws made on the factory floor along with other machine parts to make sure they were the right size and shape. He looked around at his colleagues in the quality control department.

"Some of those guys," Hanes recalls, "had sat in that inspection department for thirty years." The idea that he might be sitting there when he was fifty filled him with gloom.

"Those guys thought it was a good job," he tells me. And maybe it was—for his colleagues. But he had other ideas.

Where had he gotten those ideas? What caused him to possess, in a way that wasn't true for the seventeen other students in his high school graduating class, a sense of possibilities, of different dreams and as-yet-unseen horizons? Did he entertain the notion, even briefly, of what his future might hold? Did he think he could one day earn a doctoral degree in industrial engineering at the Ohio State University and do work he loved and live in places like Palo Alto, California?

Because he did all those things.

First, though, he had to quit.

"In that area, when you graduated from high school, you either went into the service or to the farm or a factory," Hanes recalls. "If I'd stayed, I would've married a local girl. That's what everyone did."

Not him. Because he resigned from his job. And by doing that, he was able to live another kind of life. He served in the US Air Force, married a woman named Phyllis. They raised four children as he worked for major corporations. He was part of the team that developed the first grocery store scanner. He still works as a business consultant. He and his wife divide their time between Ohio and Florida.

Hanes, a taciturn man, says he doesn't know how he found the initiative to quit his job in the summer of 1950, to walk away from a steady paycheck and opt instead to enroll at Ohio State. Not a single one of his classmates went to college. He didn't feel pressure from his mother or his teachers or anyone else in his small town to do so, he says.

Hanes's inability to articulate how he decided to quit that first job is not as surprising as it sounds. Making decisions is a complex process in ways we're only beginning to understand, according to Dr. Eric J. Johnson, author of *The Elements of Choice: Why the Way*

We Decide Matters. What once seemed like a simple binary—yes or no, stay or go—is just the outward manifestation of interlocking systems of information processing and nuances of personality, says Johnson, whose book explores what he calls "a revolution in decision research," encompassing concepts like choice architecture and assembled preferences.

"Decision-making is tough," writes Johnson, professor of marketing at Columbia University and co-director of the Center for Decision Sciences. "Sometimes we think we know what we want, but often we are faced with a situation that is not exactly like anything we have dealt with before. You might think choice is about knowing what is desirable and then locating it. In fact, the hard part is often deciding *what* we want. To do that, we review our experiences to retrieve relevant memories."

 WHITE FLAG MOMENTS

A lot of my decisions I think of as good accidents. I fell into things. But that also means I fell *out* of things. I used to play string bass in various bands. I abandoned that to go to grad school. My default was, "Well, maybe I'll get a job programming because I'm good at that." But I met the right people and they steered me toward graduate school.

—*Eric J. Johnson*

When Hanes stood at the crossroads of his life that summer after high school graduation, his hands scratched and callused from tasseling corn for a neighbor's farm—that's what he did when he wasn't working at the factory—he had a choice to make. He could inspect screws in the quality control department of the Perry-Fay plant for eight hours a day, every day, doing what the people all around him were doing—and, in fact, what most of the people he'd ever known in his life had done, if they weren't working on a farm. Or he could quit.

His decision to leave one path for another meant seeing his life differently from the way they saw theirs. And never looking back.

In the hierarchy of authority figures, it's tough to top the one who influenced Susan Warren to give up one kind of life and head for another: God.

After a successful career as an editor and writer, she decided to enroll in seminary at the age of fifty. At sixty, she became the first female minister at a church in suburban Lexington, Kentucky.

"It took a while for me to make the leap into 'This is what I'm going to do,'" she tells me. "I had been raised Presbyterian but I had misgivings about church. And then I began having a mortality crisis. I thought, 'Well, maybe I ought to figure this out.' I thought maybe I'd be a social worker. I was curious about God, though. And the more you study, the more you realize that nobody knows. A million different theories—but nobody knows. And that's okay."

Her husband and her two daughters were supportive of her decision, but friends and other family members were skeptical, she recalls. "One of my best friends said, 'What are you *thinking?*' A lot of people from my old life said, 'Susan's doing *what?*'"

Among her proudest and most satisfying moments in the new gig, she says, was the day she officiated at her church's first same-sex marriage. But there were unhappy days as well, days when she struggled, days when she wondered if quitting her former life was the right move, after all. "I went through a difficult time at first. They didn't like me," she concedes. "We lost members."

 WHITE FLAG MOMENT

It wasn't anything I'd ever thought I'd do. And then I had a conversation with a minister to check out the seminary. He asked me a lot of questions. I drove home from that meeting. It was a beautiful spring day. I went in the house and threw down my keys and went for a walk. I just felt, "Wow. This is *amazing*." I had this realization that this was something I should pursue. Everything looked vibrant and clear and beautiful—the flowers and the sky and the trees. I felt, "This is something I want to do." Suddenly, it was *right there.*

—*Susan Warren*

Gradually things turned around. Sunday by Sunday, the pews began to fill. To her surprise, pastoral counseling became one of her favorite parts of the job, although initially it was a challenge for her. She began to relish conversations with people who had big questions about their lives and about how to best serve their faith. Quitting is often the topic foremost on the minds of her parishioners—and she never minces words, Warren says.

"It comes up all the time in marriage counseling—definitely. And if it's a woman in an abusive relationship, I instinctively say, 'Get the hell out!'"

Marge Galloway is no pushover. During her thirty-two years of teaching at middle schools in Texas and Japan and Ohio, she had a reputation, I'd been told, as a formidable English teacher, the kind who held her students to high standards and demanded excellence.

That's why I'm surprised to hear that when someone wanted to quit, she'd often reply, "Okay."

Okay?

Not "Are you kidding? You march right back to your desk and you finish that assignment!" or " 'Quit'? I'm going to pretend I didn't hear you say that word. It's forbidden in this classroom."

Galloway shakes her head at my scenarios. "I never believed in just letting someone struggle through an assignment while I sat back and watched," she tells me. "I'd prefer to say, 'Let's see what we can do here.' "

Not that she doesn't believe in challenges. "Parents would say, 'You know, this just isn't good for his self-esteem.' I got so sick of that. I'd say, 'You build self-esteem by doing difficult things.' "

So where's the sweet spot between a recommendation to quit or a push to persevere? How can we be humane and understanding—but not coddle someone?

That's the point at which teaching—and parenting and coaching and mentoring of any kind—becomes more art than science, Galloway says.

"When a student is having a hard time, I would never say to a parent, 'Don't let them quit.' That wouldn't be my knee-jerk reaction. Every situation is different. Every student is different."

One young man, she recalls, was doing his best with a reading assignment that was simply beyond his capacity. "His mother called me that night and said, 'I know him. He's going to stay up all night working on this.' Well, that wasn't a good idea. So I said, 'Tell him to read until ten. And then he can stop.' "

WHITE FLAG MOMENT

There was a tense evening sitting around the dining room table. I was thirty-two. Older than the typical Peace Corps volunteer. But I was feeling a little restless. One of my family members said, "You're at the prime age to get married and have kids. And you're going to run off to Africa?" It was a big argument. But I wanted to get out in the world.

—*Lara Weber*

Quitting is more nuanced than people realize, Galloway believes, especially when you factor in authority figures. Students who are highly motivated might not quit when they need to, because they're afraid of disappointing a teacher, while students who are slackers and rebels might need to be cajoled and dissuaded from quitting.

"I had a student in my class for talented and gifted students who thought he wasn't doing well. He really wanted to quit but I didn't want him to. His mother came to me and said, 'All he does is put his head down and work. I feel I've lost my son.' I told her to let him quit. It wasn't worth what they were both going through."

Gail Hetzler, a friend of Galloway's, began her teaching career in a one-room schoolhouse in Michigan. Her forty-eight students ranged from kindergarten through eighth grade. "They took baths when the creek wasn't frozen," she tells me, so that I'll understand it wasn't some fancy prep school.

Later, she taught sixth-graders at a school in Columbus, Ohio. Before her retirement, she supervised student teachers at Ashland University in Ashland, Ohio. She and her late husband raised three children of their own, all of whom had different learning styles, she notes. One of her daughters is now an elementary school principal.

Hetzler often faced the Quitting Dilemma: sometimes it was a single assignment upon which students wanted to give up, but sometimes, for high school students, it was school itself. There's no such thing as a one-size-fits-all answer, she believes. Anyone who flatly demonizes quitting has probably never faced a classroom filled with young people, all possessing different personalities and interests and gifts.

"The brightest student I ever had was a boy named Todd. He *hated* school. Hated every minute he had to sit there. He didn't graduate from high school and got into some real problems. But I knew he'd be all right. When his parents came to me—they were both teachers—and told me he wanted to quit, they were very upset. I told them that once he found his spot in life, he'd be fine. And he is. He designs websites and makes tons of money and is extremely happy."

Hetzler's not advocating for anyone to quit school. She's a fervent believer in education. But she knows that we're all individuals—and that what looks to some people like giving up might be just another way of getting where you need to go.

"It was important to Todd's parents that he fit the mold. But it wasn't important to Todd."

PERMISSION SLIP

You care what other people think of you. And to an extent, you should. But no decision you ever make—including quitting—will ever meet with 100 percent approval from everyone. The people who love you want what's best for you, but only you can decide what "best" means. Quitting is about following your heart—even if you break someone else's in the process.

Chapter Ten

Quitting Out in the Open

Visibility these days seems to somehow equate
to success. Do not be afraid to disappear—from
it, from us—for a while, and see what comes
to you in the silence.

—*Michaela Coel, 2021 Emmy Awards ceremony*

The headline—"Girl, Wash Your Timeline"—is a bit on the
snarky side, but there's no denying that the label on the
April 29, 2021, *New York Times* article perfectly captures a central
dilemma of quitting in the contemporary world—a world domi-
nated by social media and its judgment-heavy swarms of comment
threads, gyrating GIFs, frowny faces, and the icky ubiquity of the
plain old "You suck!"

The *Times* story traces the rise and fall of Rachel Hollis, self-
improvement guru, motivational speaker, and author of *Girl, Wash
Your Face* (2018) and *Girl, Stop Apologizing* (2019), best-selling self-
help books that catapulted Hollis to wealth and fame. You can see
why the *Times* went with the clever headline: Hollis had used social
media with great skill as she created her empire of books, blog, daily
livestreams, podcasts, and line of personal care products—and yet

when things began to go wrong for the perky entrepreneur, it was social media that turned on her with fury and scorn.

The same fate awaits anybody who uses social media—which means, most likely, you and everyone you know. The ritual of quitting has been changed forever. It's no longer something that you commemorate after midnight with the curtains closed, sitting on the couch in sweats and a T-shirt, a half-eaten pint of Ben & Jerry's Cherry Garcia melting on the coffee table, sobbing into the phone while your best friend on the other end of the call murmurs, *It was about time you kicked him out. You're too good for that bastard.* Nowadays, quitting is often public. On social media, you're always in the glare of high noon.

Which is exactly what Hollis discovered. As the *Times* piece recounts, in 2020 she was forced to postpone a major conference and lost at least a hundred thousand Instagram followers. Some ill-advised social media posts had caused her devotees to question her authenticity as a champion of everyday women. And then there was the announcement that Hollis and her husband were divorcing. That didn't sit well with her fans, many of whom are married Christian women who had cherished her upbeat advice about how to keep the romance in a relationship.

None of Hollis's missteps was anywhere close to the kinds of stumbles that landed celebrities in hot water in bygone days: drug busts, sleazy affairs, drunken orgies, embezzlement, even murder. But the degree of her alleged offenses didn't seem to matter. They were very public mistakes—and so the public arena was where the punishment must occur. Her fan base was angry and their posts on Hollis's sites reflected it, forcing her withdrawal from planned events.

Live by social media, die by social media.

Few of us run multi-million-dollar wellness empires. But all of us live in an age where "public life"—a phrase formerly applicable only to politicians and celebrities—is a blanket term that can be extended to anyone with a Wi-Fi connection and a yarn to spin. Our decisions to give up on jobs, marriages, favorite bands, or political parties—decisions of which previously only a few close friends or family members might be aware—can go global with a single click, thanks to our social media accounts. And that, in turn, makes us vulnerable to the judgments of strangers and friends alike. In a nasty nanosecond, we can be unfollowed, deleted, erased, and commented about in an unpleasant way.

And while it's true that we bring a lot of this on ourselves—after all, we don't *have* to share on Facebook or Instagram—it's also true that social media is impossible to ignore as a force in the world. Social media never sleeps. Everything is scrutinized. If *you* don't comment on changes in your life status—ending or starting a relationship, moving to a new house or apartment, adopting a new dog or losing an old one—chances are, somebody else will.

So even if you're not Rachel Hollis—or Margaret Atwood or Kim Kardashian or Pink—you're affected by the change. Because public quitting has been democratized. For the obscure as well as the famous, the Internet enables a new means of living out in the open—which means, by extension, a new means of quitting out in the open.

The results are both negative and positive. Having a herd of people comment on your choices can be disconcerting, even embarrassing. Social media intensifies the experience of being judged, as Cathy O'Neil writes in *The Shame Machine: Who Profits in the New Age of Humiliation*: "Today a single slip can send the networked shame machinery into overdrive, turning it into a global event. Egged on by algorithms, millions of us participate in these dramas, providing the tech giants with free labor."

On the other hand, among the benefits of quitting in the spotlight is this: it has created a new subgenre of worker empowerment.

By the middle of 2021, it was officially a thing: quitting your job on TikTok. It was so big, in fact, that the nickname QuitTok was coined. "Wanting to quit a job" and similar phrases became trending categories. People create quick videos of themselves— sometimes playful, sometimes angry—as they resign, often in the literal moment of walking out the door. It's quite a change from the usual top-down hierarchy of the workplace, where the boss always gets the last word.

And it's not just hourly workers who use social media to quit on a public stage. On February 4, 2010, Sun Microsystems CEO Jonathan Schwartz resigned via Twitter: "Today's my last day at Sun. I'll miss it. Seems only fitting to end on a #haiku" he said in a tweet, followed by this: "Financial crisis / Stalled too many customers / CEO no more."

There are a lot of things to like about the ability to control the public narrative of our own lives. When college athletes switch schools, they don't have to let the possibly disgruntled ex-coach take charge of the announcement. Ashley Owusu, a basketball player at the University of Maryland, broke the news last year that she was transferring to Virginia Tech by posting it on her Instagram account: "I have never started anything I haven't finished, and finishing was the plan," she wrote. "Unfortunately, events that have transpired on and off the court this year have led me to make the difficult but necessary decision to continue my education and basketball career elsewhere." She chose what she wanted to say and how and when to say it, instead of letting someone else make those decisions.

But pitfalls lurk in this new reality where social media rules, says Dr. Aaron Balick, British psychotherapist and author of *The Psychodynamics of Social Networking* (2014). "Social media enables identities to become more fixed," he tells me. "One's public identity on social media may compromise the decision-making process to persevere or to quit due to the investment into one's own identity."

If you've reinforced a certain view of yourself by frequent postings on social media, then changing that identity—say, quitting a job you claimed to have loved or a relationship that you'd presented as perfect—might be more difficult, he notes. Social media "may pressure the individual to move toward one solution over the other." Instead of following your heart—or even your common sense—when you're making up your mind about your next move, you may be anticipating the reaction you'll receive to that post. Hence, it's not *you* who's really doing the deciding—it's other people. And is checking the result of an unofficial online poll really the best way to run your life?

Through our online presence we create an identity, an ongoing narrative about our lives, Balick says. The act of quitting requires us to either change that narrative or decide not to. "Persevering is almost always the default position—to quit takes a different kind of action," he adds. Quitting is "simply a choice to make...There is no essential value in quitting or staying—it's the narrative you and others bring to that decision."

Ah, those were the days: A politician storming off during a live interview. A celebrity calling a press conference to announce an impending departure from a film project. That's how it used to be done by people in the public eye.

Some lingering traces of the old-fashioned way of public quitting do remain, reminding us of how much the world has changed. On the morning of January 12, 2022, National Public Radio anchor Steve Inskeep had been promised a fifteen-minute interview with Donald Trump. Things started out fine. Nine minutes in, though, after some verbal volleys back and forth over the forty-fifth president's continued insistence that the 2020 election was filched from him, Trump apparently had had enough. Abruptly, he said, "So Steve, thank you very much. I appreciate it."

And with that, he left.

A few seconds passed before Inskeep, having launched into his next question, realized that he was talking to himself now. "He's gone. Okay," he said, his tone one of puzzled rue more than bristling, how-could-he-do-that-to-me irritation.

This wasn't the first time Trump had called it quits in midinterview. On October 20, 2020, he grew visibly annoyed at *60 Minutes* anchor Lesley Stahl's questions and—*whoosh*—he was gone. Nor is he the originator of this gesture, this public way of extricating oneself from a situation one has decided no longer suits. Politicians just happen to be especially fond of it. There's a long tradition of public figures ripping off lapel mics and yanking out earbuds just prior to slamming away from a TV set while muttering, "I refuse to dignify that rubbish with a reply!" or similar spittle-flecked umbrage. Celebrities from the worlds of entertainment, sports, and business do it as well, making their getaways from uncomfortable venues when the lights are bright and the mics are hot.

Another way to quit in public, to exit in the blinding glare of media scrutiny, is to be a whistleblower. In October 2021, former Facebook employee Frances Haugen testified for four days before a US Senate committee about what she believes is the company's indifference to the distress caused by its algorithms. On her way out the door after working at Facebook for some two years, she'd taken data that she hoped would prove her case.

"I'm here today because I believe Facebook's products harm children, stoke division and weaken our democracy," Haugen told the legislators. "The company's leadership knows how to make Facebook and Instagram safer, but won't make the necessary changes because they have put their astronomical profits before people." She left her job, that is, with a very public repudiation of her former employers.

Not all whistleblowers take the public route, as Patrick Radden Keefe notes in his 2022 *New Yorker* article about a federal program that financially rewards insiders who report potential corporate crimes on their way out the door. There's no requirement to tell the world in order to have charges taken seriously. "Some elect not to go public," Keefe writes. But when someone like Haugen quits and makes explosive allegations at a congressional hearing, she turns leaving into an act of courage; retaliation seems like a very real threat. By disclosing publicly the information that she did, she made her quitting matter.

———

Quitting in public doesn't have to be an angry, obscenity-rich rant at a bad boss or a revelation about allegedly nefarious business practices. It doesn't have to highlight something unpleasant. People post videos from retirement parties and selfies from bucket-list trips on Facebook and Instagram. You can quit one kind of life for another in a public way—and it can be about sharing, not score settling.

When Melissa Allison decided to remarry, she was filled with joy and hope—and a touch of trepidation. She'd been married previously to a man she still loved and respected. Before she left the relationship, there had been no outward signs of tension. Many of the friends with whom she wasn't in regular touch wouldn't know what had happened. She didn't have the time or energy to send out scads of texts. A group email seemed too cold and scattershot.

Word might reach her friends anyway, through the natural course of human behavior—i.e., gossip—but that didn't much appeal to her, either. She wanted to tell her own story, to inform hundreds of people—all at once—that she'd quit her old life. What could she do?

The answer was easy, Allison said: Facebook.

But this part was harder: waiting for the responses to the text and photos of her and Deborah, her new partner, at their oceanside ceremony.

"The Facebook post was scary," Allison admits. "I had a little practice telling people—close friends in person, immediate family by phone, extended family by email—and knew that Facebook might be cruel, as it's a broader group and can sometimes be judgmental. But I took the same approach as I had elsewhere and was relieved to find that the people I'm in touch with on Facebook are not judgmental. It was a relief to finally have it out there broadly, and the awkward questions stopped trickling in."

Allison, who works for a real estate company in Seattle, had been married for many years when she met Deborah at a spiritual retreat. Of her relationship with her ex-husband, she says, "It wasn't awful. It just wasn't life-giving. I thought, 'There's got to be more.'"

Yet quitting her marriage to marry Deborah was a wrenching decision, Allison tells me. "I have a lot of guilt about it. But the relationship hadn't felt right for a long time. As soon as I realized that, I started to emerge. To know what life meant to me."

In the early days of her discontent, she thought that perhaps quitting her job would settle her down. Then she realized the problem ran deeper. It was personal, not professional.

WHITE FLAG MOMENT

I loved my cats. I loved Seattle. I thought, "Why am I continually seeking?" In that moment, I found myself. I got myself. The pain I felt from not doing what I needed to do for myself would rise up. I changed—in a moment.

—*Melissa Allison*

After the ceremony—photos of which adorn her Facebook page—she and her wife bought a house in Hawaii, where Allison works remotely. When the workday is over, they're apt to go snorkeling, spend time with their two cats and a dog, or tend to the garden, where they grow pineapples, papayas, bananas, avocados, and oranges.

Quitting a marriage and embarking upon another so publicly is risky, she admits. "I'm a 'divorced person.' I never thought I'd wear that label. But when people tie that stuff to you, they're just mimicking some bullshit that culture taught them. And it's not tied to anything real."

———

Even as noncelebrities increasingly indulge in public quitting, famous people haven't given up the practice, either. The tradition of exiting a live interview with theatrical rage is alive and well—and as obnoxious as ever:

"I have been assassinated! Buried alive! But I'm alive!"

That was R. Kelly, the disgraced singer convicted in 2021 of crimes including racketeering, bribery, and sexual exploitation, during his interview with Gayle King on *CBS News* on March 6, 2019. His outburst continued: "I didn't do this stuff. This is not me...I'm fighting for my fucking life. You're all trying to kill me!" He abandoned the interview in an angry huff, lurching off the set.

The possibility of public quitting is woven into the culture of the live TV or radio interview, a huge part of its allure. We have to watch or listen because we just *know* something's going to happen—something dramatic, maybe something dangerous, but definitely something you'll be talking about with your friends and colleagues tomorrow.

But what makes it so appealing for us, beyond the fun of pure spectacle? Perhaps it's the fact that, despite the inevitability of the subjects' reaction to blunt questions—did anyone really think R. Kelly would stick around for King's inquiries about the allegations he faced, or that Trump would hang out for long with an NPR host?—there is something inherently transgressive about giving up, and something *doubly* transgressive about giving up in plain sight. Not one but *two* traditional bulwarks of culture are being breached: the idea that you shouldn't quit, and the idea that if you do, you should do it quietly.

We're drawn over and over again to the vivid ending, to the public severing of ties, both as voyeurs and as practitioners.

But are there any unofficial rules for online quitting?

The Internet is rightly celebrated as a gloriously free and unfettered place where the only rule is that there *are* no rules, where normal social niceties don't have to be observed—in fact, they are meant to be subverted. That anarchy is a big part of the charm: not knowing what's going to happen next creates a constantly renewed frisson of excitement. But the next time you're tempted to tell the world—on your way out the door for the last time—that your boss is a bastard or your partner is a cheating bum, you might want to consider a couple of guiding principles for your own public quitting:

First, be like Edward, not Richard.

And second, know when to quit on public quitting.

––––––––––––

If a twenty-first-century monarch needs to tell their subjects that they're quitting, Twitter is the go-to venue. Lacking that option in 1936, Great Britain's King Edward VIII sat down at a desk in Windsor Castle on a momentous day, pulled the large microphone closer, the one that would broadcast his words to radio listeners throughout his kingdom, and spoke slowly and solemnly but with determination: "A few hours ago I discharged my last duties as king and emperor." In what he called "the most serious decision of my life," he declared that he was giving up the throne to marry Wallis Simpson, an American woman who, as a divorcée, could never be queen.

Compare Edward's eloquence to another pre-Internet episode of public quitting: the first of Richard Nixon's two televised resignations, a self-pity-fueled fit of pique during a press conference on November 7, 1962, after his loss in the California gubernatorial race. The subtext of the message from this future president of the United States could have come just as readily from a minimum-wage worker posting a kiss-off video on TikTok: *What—you think I won't do it? Watch me. I'm so gonna go public.*

To the reporters assembled at the Beverly Hilton Hotel that day, a clearly hacked-off Nixon declared, "You don't have Nixon to kick around anymore, gentlemen. This is my last press conference. Thank you, gentlemen, and good day."

Given that sullen and sulky goodbye, how did Nixon ever return to public life? Timing was the key, says Robert Schmuhl, presidential historian and emeritus professor of American studies at the University of Notre Dame. "So much happened between his so-called last press conference following the California gubernatorial loss in 1962 that by 1968 the earlier defeat and what he said afterwards didn't seem to matter all that much," Schmuhl tells me. "The country had endured the assassination of John Kennedy, the deadly difficulties of the Vietnam War, the decline of Lyndon Johnson's presidency, the killings of Martin Luther King and Senator Robert Kennedy, the riots in several cities, and all the rest."

Another factor that prevented Nixon's public quitting moment from harming his image is that few people actually saw it live or saw it at all, Schmuhl adds. "It's important to remember that at the time there were no half-hour network news programs. Those didn't come until a year later. Moreover, the country wasn't as saturated back then as it's been since the 1980s in television news and video images. There was film of what Nixon said, but there wasn't anything like the repetition that exists now. Print journalism was much more significant back then, and reading the former vice president's statements would never be the same as seeing and hearing them."

The spectacle of the public quit—that riveting visual of a grown man losing his cool—is what made the moment sizzle. A transcript can't hold a candle to the live event. Nixon was fortunate that he threw his sore-loser tantrum in a time before Twitter. Otherwise, he'd have been crushed by the sheer tonnage of all those comment threads.

By the time he quit in public for the second time—August 8, 1974, when he resigned the presidency in the wake of the Watergate scandal—the media landscape had been completely transformed. Millions watched the TV networks' news bulletin featuring his resignation.

Yet even at that grave historical moment, with so many watching and so much at stake for the nation and the world, Nixon was still extra sensitive about one thing: the implication that he wasn't tough enough to stick it out. Call him a liar, call him a cad, call him an unscrupulous manipulator, call him anything you like—just don't call him...well, you know. To him, no insult was worse.

With steel in his voice, Nixon declared, "I have never been a quitter."

The second tip is about timing. Granted, the urge to share a change in your life and to engage with a multitude of followers can be irresistible. "Twitter is a red light, blinking, blinking, blinking," writes Caitlin Flanagan in a funny-because-it's-true essay about her attempt to quit Twitter cold turkey for twenty-eight days. "Twitter is a parasite that burrows deep in your brain, training you to respond to the constant social feedback of likes and retweets."

Strong is the temptation to let everyone know about your life decisions, from breakups to resignations to that pulled hamstring that kept you out of CrossFit for a month. A bit of restraint, though, might be warranted, despite the fact that we're part of a society "used to living their life in full view," writes Moya Lothian-McLean in an essay titled "I Built a Life on Oversharing—Until I Saw Its Costs, and Learned the Quiet Thrill of Privacy." She adds, "Sharing became how I made my own life real." Only recently did she learn the thrill of *not* sharing everything online: It constitutes "a reclamation of power I wasn't aware I'd surrendered." Once you *do* realize how much of your core self you've given up to public sharing of every detail of your life, you may want to step back. And be more sparing and judicious about what you post.

As Lothian-McLean notes, "There is a burgeoning backlash against oversharing, counting Taylor Swift and some UK teens among its converts."

Maybe it's time to rethink the idea that everything has to be on the table for others to comment on, from what you do to what you decide to stop doing. Granted, it won't be a snap. The social bias against quitting sometimes makes us more, not less, inclined to share it too often—and with too many people—because challenging authority is a basic human drive. We don't like being defined by other people's ideas of what makes a successful life. We want to make those decisions for ourselves, decisions about when to stay and when to go. And so we may react a little overenthusiastically to the freedom of the online world. Liberated at last from pandemic lockdowns, still getting used to the idea of being part of the larger world, we're apt to be too open rather than excessively guarded, too candid instead of overly discreet.

Adele, the British singer who's always been forthright with her fans about her struggles with body image and intimacy, talks a lot about her divorce across multiple platforms. She gives her new status a positive spin, a habit that irritates her countrywoman Freya India. "These days," India complained in a *Spectator* essay, "divorce is seen as just another form of self-empowerment. Divorce must not be seen as a tragedy, it seems; it's a cause for celebration, a much deserved do-over." But India misses the point of the singer's insistence on social media and in interviews that she and her child are doing fine. Adele is publicly upbeat about quitting her decade-long relationship, I think, because in years past, the world expected a divorced woman to grieve in private, to mourn, to cower, to go off and hide as if her life were over. Instead, the entertainer gushes openly and often about her joy after the breakup.

Adele's public quitting is her retort to that sexist standard, her way of saying to the world, in essence, "I'm good, thanks. The decision about how and with whom I'm going to live—and what makes me happy—is *mine*, not yours." Quitting out in the open might not be the best choice in all circumstances, but the point is, you get to do the choosing.

PERMISSION SLIP

You enjoy sharing what's going on in your life. That can include the news of important decisions you make about jobs, school, relationships. But social media raises the stakes on quitting. Don't let it trick you into telling the world anything before you're ready.

_____

Chapter Eleven

A Community of Quitters

Giving up hope has given me back the
capacity for joy.

—*Keith Kahn-Harris*

A my Dickinson likes people. That's a good thing, as it happens, because her job as a syndicated advice columnist is to listen to us complain about our lives, from our petty irritations to our overwhelming sorrows to the minor disappointments and annoyances in between, and to remind us that we're all in the same boat: being human. And it can get pretty choppy out there, for all of us.

Due to the aforesaid affection for the human species, Dickinson longs to be part of something bigger than just herself, part of a larger whole. It was therefore no surprise that when they asked her to join their organization, her answer was a quick and grateful affirmative.

So why did she then turn around and quit?

"Honestly, I don't think I had ever quit *anything* until June 9, 2020," she tells me. "It was the day of George Floyd's funeral and I chose to resign my membership in the Daughters of the American Revolution. I had been admitted—with major fanfare—as their one millionth member a few months before." A "national media blitz" had been planned, she adds, to publicize her shiny new status as a DAR member.

You can understand why the DAR would want Dickinson on the team. She writes a column that runs in periodicals nationwide, her books are bestsellers, she's a regular on National Public Radio. She's a vivid, captivating speaker with a large and devoted following. But between her "yes" and the kickoff of the publicity tour, she'd been heartbroken and outraged by Floyd's murder, and sickened by the racism that prompted it. So she told the organization that, as their newest member, she'd be discussing publicly the group's troubling historical record on race.

That record included the moment on Easter Sunday 1939 when the DAR refused to allow Black contralto Marian Anderson to sing at Constitution Hall because of a "whites only" clause in their artists' contracts. In an electric moment in the long history of the fight for racial justice in America, Anderson sang "My Country 'Tis of Thee" at the Lincoln Memorial instead, thrilling the thousands who thronged there to hear her.

"I believed they needed to continue to examine their history through this lens—it is, after all, an organization obsessed with history," Dickinson says. "The president of the organization did not like that at all." After a bit more back-and-forth, Dickinson still wasn't satisfied with their response to the racial justice reckoning that was sweeping the country. "History forced my hand and made it very easy for me to resign. I probably should never have joined in the first place," Dickinson goes on. "But like a lot of people who can't quit anything, I tend to obligate myself to things because I don't have the confidence to decline.

"Quitting that, I got a taste of the liberation that can flow from quitting."

Next up on her Quit Parade: an online book club that she'd

been trying to leave for six months. "I didn't really have time for the Zoom meetings. But mainly, I just didn't enjoy it. I was tempted to offer up a bunch of fibs and excuses about why I was quitting. Instead, I just told them I didn't want to do it anymore."

Dickinson's foot-dragging on quitting—even when she knew it was the right move to make—wasn't simple avoidance of an unpleasant task. There's another factor at work here: when you quit, you're leaving a community. Communities supply us with a context for our lives and with a sense of ourselves as more than just separate pieces of humanity, drifting around the universe. They provide a kind of binding glue. They give us a connection, a tether. As single entities, it's almost as if we're too light, too insubstantial; there's a chance we might fly right off the face of the earth. To decide to quit is to set yourself free, yes, but it's also to lose that grounding, the essential ballast of others. Sometimes that ballast is a drag; other times, a comfort. "Unattached" is a concept that cuts both ways.

"With quitting, you're putting yourself out of the group," Leidy Klotz tells me. He's the University of Virginia professor who wrote *Subtract: The Untapped Science of Less.* "You're no longer in the group and you risk being stigmatized."

Buried in the word "decide" is the violence of severance. The Latin root of the second syllable refers to the killing of other options. (Just as "regicide" is killing a king, "homicide" killing a person, "pesticide" is bug killer, and "suicide" killing oneself.) Deciding to quit can bring relief and satisfaction, as it did for Dickinson. But sometimes it can also bring regret and second thoughts—right away or, as we shall see, years later.

You're on the outside now. You're no longer one of the gang.

When we quit—when we leave a gig, a sidekick, a home, a team,

a relationship, a religious belief, a business idea—we don't just abandon an activity, a person, a hope, or a seat at the table. We also lose
the kinship with others. It's why people who could easily watch a
football game on an HDTV set at home in their flannel jammies
and fuzzy slippers still traipse out to the stadium on a freezing night
to sit in the cold and get their shoes ruined by stepping in puddles
of spilled beer.

It feels good to nestle down inside something that's bigger (and
louder and rowdier) than you could possibly be by yourself. Quitting
means letting go of that comfort. And while it may leave you feeling
unburdened, it also can leave you feeling lonely. You're no longer on
the membership roll, or listed on the company website with a head-
shot and a short bio.

Maybe that's why we hesitate to quit things that we know aren't
helping us, things that may, in fact, definitely be harming us. Every
decision to quit is a move away from the familiar and the predictable
and toward the new, the strange, the possibly perilous.

It might work out magnificently. And it might not.

Quitting is not only about what you're giving up. It's also about
the wilderness in which you find yourself postquit. You lose the con-
solation of context. And while you gain another context, for the first
bit of time you might feel lost. Unmoored, even. Because you don't
belong anymore.

When we quit, we lose a connection with others. But the good
news is that in the wake of that loss, we make other connections. As
Bessel van der Kolk reminds us in *The Body Keeps the Score*, "Our
culture teaches us to focus on personal uniqueness, but at a deeper
level we barely exist as individual organisms. Our brains are built to
help us function as members of a tribe."

Thus, quitting is an emotional and spiritual challenge as well as
a logistical one, Connie Schultz tells me. In her career as a Pulitzer

Prize–winning columnist, first with the Cleveland *Plain Dealer* and now with *USA Today*, she's interviewed many people about their lives. Those conversations have persuaded her that there are different kinds of quitting, and that each calls for a separate kind of courage.

You can quit a job, but a job is only one part of life. Another type of quitting means leaving behind the current version of who you are—because it doesn't match up with who you've always wanted to be.

 WHITE FLAG MOMENT

By the time I physically left, I was already emotionally gone. I was doing good work, but I was doing it in isolation...I'm different inside from having left the *Plain Dealer*. I wouldn't want to go back to who I was before I left. I was more fearful. I didn't see my world in as big a way as I do now. Quitting helped me become a better friend to people. A better mentor to my students. When you go through something, you learn from it and pass it on.

—*Connie Schultz*

"If we need to make a job change, we can do that," she says. "But if what needs to change is the personal undergirding, that's harder. To bring in new people, new experiences, we have to create space for it. If that space is being taken up by people who make you feel defensive or inferior, there's no room for the change." Schultz knows a great deal about change and possibility, about all the different spaces one person can fill in the world: not only is she a journalist and best-selling novelist, she's also a college professor, a mother, a grandmother, and the wife of United States senator Sherrod Brown.

Until we walk away from the parts of our lives that aren't working, "there's no energy left for something new to find us. We only get so much energy every day." Of the second kind of quitting, Schultz has this to say: "It's much quieter. Much softer. It's the ability to dream of something bigger."

———————

Patty Bills is well acquainted with dreams and how they can inspire major life changes. Eight years ago, she gave up her job with the federal government to be a full-time artist. That job had featured a good salary and benefits and security.

There was just one small hitch, Bills recalls: "It was killing my soul."

She and her husband, Thomas, moved to eastern Wyoming a dozen years ago. They loved the place, loved the rugged landscape, loved the fact that no two sunrises were ever the same. But she wasn't crazy about her work as an administrator for the US Forest Service, handling fleet management.

Bills took a pottery class and discovered she had a passion for it, for designing mugs and cups and plates and trays and vases, for hand-painting original wildlife scenes on them and firing the glaze. You'll see moose and trout on Bills's work, and soaring birds and curious bears.

In 2015, like one of those trout she's painted on plenty of mugs, capturing the moment that it leaps up from the frothy water, she, too, made a big jump.

"The job stress and my dislike of it was growing and so I quit. I became a full-time potter," she tells me. "I just made up my mind that I was done." Any jitters before she handed in her notice? "That same paycheck every two weeks—you get used to it. And we had a mortgage. And a thirteen-year-old child. So yes—I was scared. But my pottery was selling. I thought, 'I could do this as a business. I really could.'"

 WHITE FLAG MOMENT

I made up my mind that I was done. I told my parents I was quitting my job. I told them, "I can't do it anymore. It's just too stressful." My parents said, "Oh, Tricia, you really should think this through." I said, "I have. I have." Two weeks after I left that job, my daughter said, "I got my mom back."

—*Patty Bills*

Even before her resignation, Bills had begun to offer her work on consignment to galleries and gift shops across the West. Her work sold well right out of the gate. So yes—she took a risk, but a calculated one. She enrolled in courses about how to run a business. She understood that making a living at her art was going to require more than just talent. She had to be an entrepreneur as well as an artist.

The pandemic was rough, she says. "Oh, so depressing. No shows or artist-in-residences, galleries and shops closed." Her website and Facebook page enabled her to continue selling her work. But it was a daunting time.

And then the world began to open up again. "Right now, I'm struggling to keep up with gallery orders and shows," she reports. "I love my career. You're working with clay—with a piece of the earth." She laughs. "Sometimes I'm really grateful for that last straw in my government job."

The lesson? "Sometimes we have to get out of our own heads and stop putting numbers down on paper. I'd never be here if I hadn't taken that leap. That leap is scary and you're afraid of it. But there can be so much joy in it."

Growing up in Evanston, Illinois, Tim Bannon, former features editor at the *Chicago Tribune*, was a fine athlete. He was tall and agile, with a strong kicking leg. He played soccer and rugby in high school. And so in his freshman year at Miami University in Oxford, Ohio, he decided to try for a spot on the football team as a kicker, even though he didn't have a scholarship. He wrote a note to the head coach, Dick Crum, promising that he could drill fifty-yard kicks through the uprights.

"Within the hour," Bannon recalls, "my dorm phone rings. It's Dick Crum. He says, 'Come show me what you can do.' It was me and the entire coaching squad on the field. I was nailing these kicks right and left. He said, 'That's great, kid. You're on the team.' It was such a whirlwind after that."

At the first practice with the whole team present, Crum turned to his new kicker: " 'Bannon!' he yells. 'Get in there!' I'd never had eleven guys facing me, seven yards away. First one—boom. I kicked it into the center's back."

Subsequent kicks were equally embarrassing. Bannon had the physical skills—but not the mindset. "There's something singular about kicking. It all comes down to the kicker. You're by yourself. You have to learn to deal with that attention."

A few weeks later, "after wallowing on the sidelines," he quit the team. That season—1975–76—was a memorable one for Miami football. The team ended up ranked in the top twenty in the nation. He would've been a part of that.

"It's one of the things I have regret for. I didn't realize the incredible opportunity I had—writing a letter to the coach, getting on one of the best teams in the nation. My life would've gone in a whole other direction. I'm happy for the direction it *did* go—but it would've been different. I regret that I didn't try a little harder before I gave up."

Perhaps we don't quit as often as we should. Perhaps quitting is unfairly stigmatized. But it's also true that the decision to give up may haunt us henceforth. We may always wonder:

What if?

In the years that followed, Bannon put the memory of his quitting moment to good use in his parenting, he tells me. He and his wife have raised three children. And when his kids wanted to quit something—a sports team, a musical instrument, a hobby—he had a conversation with them. "Because of my decision to quit that team, I was less likely to just let them off. I'd work through it with them. 'Let's talk about *why* you feel this way.' I was more sensitive to them quitting something."

Bannon may wish he'd stayed, but other people may wish they'd left. The nonquit, that is, can haunt you just as much as the quit. In his novel *The Only Story*, Julian Barnes offers this bittersweet scenario from the other side and shows what happens when we don't quit something we should because quitting is inconvenient:

> Over my life I've seen friends fail to leave their marriages, fail to continue their affairs, fail even to start them sometimes, all for the same expressed reason. "It just isn't practical," they say wearily. The distances are too great, the train schedules unfavourable, the work hours mismatched; then there's the mortgage; and the children, and the dog; also the joint ownership of things. "I just couldn't face sorting out the record collection," a non-leaving wife once told me.

It's not about the record collection. It's about deciding where you belong and wondering, as your life unwinds to its end, if you made the right choice.

———————

Dr. Gaurava Agarwal's advice boils down to this: think beyond the quit.

When physicians come into his office and say they're burned-out and want to quit medicine, his first response is to offer three words:

"Quit to what?"

Here's what he means. "It's one thing to quit—you have this idea that quitting's going to make it better. But *where* is it going to be better? This idyllic place of puppy dogs and rainbows—it doesn't exist," he tells me. "So I say to the people who come in, 'Quit to what?'"

Agarwal is director of Physician Well-Being for Northwestern Medical Group and director of Medical Student Education in Psychiatry at Northwestern University Feinberg School of Medicine. When doctors are stressed, frazzled, fried, fed up, and oh-so-close to flinging their stethoscopes into the nearest trash can and storming out, Agarwal is the go-to guy. He's a psychiatrist with certification as a leadership coach for health care professionals.

"I ask them, 'Is there a way to craft your career here without quitting?'"

That's because, Agarwal says, quitting can seem like a quick and easy solution to a problem that's been a long time in the making. But if the issue didn't arise in a flash, then maybe the answer to it shouldn't come that way, either.

"There's the sense that the last thing that happened is the reason you want to quit. But that's not usually the case," he says. "Usually it's from things that have built up slowly." And even the most intractable-seeming problem can be less daunting if it's discussed and dismantled, piece by piece. "People with marriage or job problems come to me and say, 'I'm done.' But then we look at it. We go through it rationally, systematically. There's a sense that people are checking out a little too early."

And if a physician tells him that she hears an inner voice urging her to quit?

"My gut tells me that voice is not all that trustworthy," Agarwal cautions. "And anyway, there are other voices, too. And maybe you should listen to those."

When the pandemic raged at its height, a daily barrage of news stories reported that health care professionals were leaving their jobs in weary droves. Agarwal points out, though, that it's always been a stressful, demanding field, pandemic or no pandemic. "People feel that it's not just a job—it's a calling. We hear the word 'resilience' a lot. But health care people aren't resilient—they're resistant. When they finally break, it's not from the last hit. It's from everything that came before." But he doesn't believe the exodus will return to its peak pandemic rate.

Quitting may sound like the perfect solution—until the future is factored in, a future minus the community of colleagues providing emotional and practical sustenance. Which is why Agarwal came up with his trademark response: "Quit to what?"

As long as the troubled physician sitting across the desk from him is stuck for an answer, he says, she doesn't really want to go. Yet if quitting does seem like the best answer, Agarwal is fine with that; he just wants the physician to make sure it's a thoughtful, carefully wrought decision and not a whim, not a frustration-fueled response to one bad day.

He's not against quitting per se. He simply believes it ought to be part of a strategy.

––––––––––

Glen Worthey and his family "rolled into town" on New Year's Eve three and a half years ago, as he describes it, after living twenty-two years in Palo Alto, California, home of Stanford University, where he worked as a digital librarian. The town into which they'd rolled was—wait for it—Champaign, Illinois, where icy winds tend to slap you around all winter long and the snow never lets up. In other words, not a palm tree in sight.

"I'd reached a plateau at Stanford and was ready for a change. I was ready for a new adventure," he tells me. "But the response I got when we first arrived here and people heard I'd been at Stanford was, 'Are you *nuts?*' A grad school friend of mine is here, though, and he'd told me that he loved the drama of the seasons. I thought he was being metaphorical. He wasn't. And now I love it, too."

The drama in Worthey's life wasn't confined to the weather report. Shortly after starting his new job as associate director of research support services at the University of Illinois, he and his wife separated.

"I was extremely hesitant to quit the marriage," he says. "I had accepted a less-than-perfect marriage that had descended into the toxic. But I've always thought of myself as having a superhuman amount of grit." And so he took a while, he says, to decide to leave the relationship.

That slow-motion uncoupling echoes a similar one earlier in his life. Worthey was raised in the Mormon faith. "I was deeply entrenched in it. I went in headfirst in every way," he remembers. His undergraduate degree is from Brigham Young University. Yet after returning from a postgraduate fellowship in Russia, he was aware of a change in himself. "Doubts were coming. I realized I don't really believe in God. But it took me a long time to identify as an atheist."

Quitting his faith meant leaving not only a system of belief, but also the social life provided by the Mormon church. His church family was an extension of his birth family; it had long given him comfort and identity. And now he was leaving all of that behind. Friends and loved ones were understanding about his decision, Worthey says, but he knew he was losing so many familiar aspects of his life, the customs and rituals and trappings. He doesn't regret leaving behind a church in whose precepts he no longer believes—but sometimes he wishes he'd quit sooner and more forthrightly, had severed the tie with a neat snip instead of going through years of reflection.

Such hesitation was entirely typical for him, he says. He's always taken his time before changing course—when he's able to do it at all.

"As an undergraduate I was a triple major in physics, English, and Russian—because I couldn't quit any of them."

———————

All of us, from time to time, are part of the Community of Quitters.

There is great sustenance to be derived from knowing about other people who have given up the same things that you have—and survived, even flourished. There is a solace to be found in joining a group you didn't even know existed until a personal crisis flings you into their ranks.

When I came across Margaret Renkl's story, I was struck by how similar it sounded to mine.

Uncannily so, right down to the Dad Rescue.

Midway through her lyrical essay collection *Late Migrations: A Natural History of Love and Loss*, I came across Renkl's brief recollection about the time she left home to go to grad school and how she hated it and was totally miserable, and so one night she called home and her father answered and...

You can maybe guess the rest of the story, because it's close to the one I told about myself in the introduction. Other than the fact that Renkl's epiphany came when she was twenty-two and mine when I was nineteen, and she was stressed out in Philadelphia while I was stressed out in Morgantown, our experiences rhymed for a time: we both found ourselves totally out of our element in grad school in a new city, distraught and confused.

It was quit or die. Or so it felt at the time.

During the day, Renkl had to listen to cynical professors who told her that literature had no meaning; once the sun went down, she was menaced by other sources.

"All night long," she writes of her dingy apartment, "the gears of delivery trucks ground at the traffic light on the corner; four floors down, strangers muttered and swore in the darkness." She missed the natural landscape of her Southern home, the birdcalls and the red soil, and I suppose I missed the particulars of my homeplace as well, although I don't think I could have articulated that at the time, as Renkl so beautifully does, because I was stupefied with sadness.

Just as I didn't stick it out, she didn't, either. She called home. Her father said, in effect, *Come on down.*

Giving up did the trick, she writes, and proved to be the gateway to the rest of her life: "I think most of my own happiness, of all the years with a good man and the family we have made together and the absorbing work—everything that followed a single season of loss, and only because I listened to my father. Because I came home."

The happy ending after she gave up wasn't assured, of course. Things might not have worked out. She might never have been admitted to another grad school (this time, in her beloved South) or met her husband or been blessed with a wonderful family or become an author and columnist for the *New York Times*.

Renkl abandoned one community—grad school in Philly—and returned to her original community, her family, and everything clicked. But she had to risk it *not* clicking. She had to take a chance on one failure following another.

Learning about Renkl's midnight flight from grad school, I felt a sense of relief, even though it's been many years since my Morgantown meltdown. I hadn't realized that I was still holding on to a tiny scrap of self-reproach, a small but annoying anxiety: Was it really okay to quit? Should I have hung in there, after all?

Then I read Renkl and was elated:

Somebody else did it, too. Somebody else was huddled in a scared lump in a small apartment in a strange city, worried that it would all go on forever, the pain and confusion. But she left, too. She broke free, too. Quitting is fine. It's a legitimate response to an emotional SOS.

————————

Quitting is the last resort. The swan song. Famous quitting scenes in movies and TV shows and novels are predicated on the dramatically rich idea that—after a steadily escalating series of frustrations and indignities—finally we blow, we crack, we explode, we lose it, we come apart at the seams. We don't think about the consequences, because we're out of control.

But does it have to be so dire? In his essay about the record number of pandemic-inspired resignations in 2021—what he calls "the summer of quitting"—Derek Thompson points out that giving up has a positive side. It all depends on who's doing the defining: "Quitting gets a bad rap in life, as it's associated with pessimism, laziness, and lack of confidence. In labor economics, however, quits signify the opposite: an optimism among workers about the future; an eagerness to do something new."

And in science, quitting is key. You can't find the correct idea if you insist on clinging to the old, incorrect one. Richard A. Muller, emeritus professor of physics at the University of California, Berkeley, has complained that non-scientists sometimes see his field as an impregnable citadel of certainty, believing erroneously that scientists rarely change their minds. "They don't realize," he told a journalist, "how much time scientists spend coming up with ideas and rejecting them." Giving up on a theory that proves to be wrong is the essential precursor to finding the accurate one—and to scientific progress in general.

I've argued that quitting can be a life strategy—and a better one, in the long run, than perseverance, because, among other things, it requires us to develop empathy for the plight of other people. Also, it calls upon a survival capacity for which our brains specifically are constructed. How, though, does that work?

George A. Bonanno, a clinical psychologist and a professor at Columbia University Teachers College, has done groundbreaking research into grief and healing. In his latest book, *The End of Trauma: How the New Science of Resilience Is Changing How We Think about PTSD*, he explores the ways by which people deal with profound emotional traumas.

When I read his book, one aspect jumped out at me: he sees quitting as an asset.

Quitting is the final step in a technique Bonanno calls flexibility sequencing. It's a vital part of the active management of an emotionally fraught situation. You can size up the moment and decide whether or not your current method for dealing with an issue is working. If it's not, then a change is in order.

You don't have to be a victim to your coping mechanism any more than you're a victim to your circumstances. When the steps you've undertaken prove ineffective, you can change them. You can quit and try something else.

"Flexibility is not a passive process," he writes. "In the wake of trauma, we have to work out the best solution moment by moment as we struggle, and then we have to readjust as we go along. In other words, we have to be flexible...We work out what is happening to us and what we can do to manage it. There is also a crucial corrective step where we determine whether a strategy we choose is working or [if] we should change to another strategy."

If we are fortunate, most of us will never have to endure the sorts of horrific traumas for which Bonanno's work attempts to provide a measure of relief: war; emotional, physical, and sexual abuse; disfiguring and disabling accidents. But I believe that his insights are applicable to many less profound challenges, too.

Quitting is a resource to be deployed. It's a decision, not a defeat. A pivot point. And it's available to us in ways we are just beginning to appreciate.

"Most people are resilient," Bonanno writes. "Most people must be flexible enough to determine what the right behavior is in a given situation and at a given time, and then be able to engage in that behavior to adapt and move forward." That involves a willingness to stop and go another way.

At the risk of oversimplifying Bonanno's layered and nuanced technique, here's a summary. In the wake of an adverse reaction to a troubling memory, ask yourself four questions: What is happening? What do I need to do? What am I able to do? And once I start doing it, is it effective?

"When a strategy is not working, feedback, either from our bodies or from the world around us, tells us that we need to modify the strategy or try something else," he writes. "It is important to point out that these are not rare abilities. They are simply underappreciated features of the human mind, and they can be nurtured and improved." The same shared survival instinct that pushes us to quit when we need to, then, may help as well when it comes to moving past debilitating events in our past. We can't change what happened to us—but we can develop a response to troubling memories and difficult situations that helps us heal and move forward.

We need to check in periodically, assessing the efficacy of our actions: Are we making progress? And were we on the right path to begin with?

———————

Quitting is a vastly underutilized resource. It's a strategy we may not recognize as a legitimate choice at all, but only as a compromise or a failure. It's an untapped source of energy and inspiration that we shun out of a misguided sense that giving up—unless you're talking about serial killing, substance abuse, or excess carbs—is inherently a bad thing. The lives of other animals—who quit constantly, as indeed they must in order to stay alive—are proof of the value of quitting, and the difference it can make.

But that doesn't mean, of course, that quitting is *always* a good thing. No single course of action is right for everyone in all circumstances. Too often, though, quitting is rejected out of hand.

And in the long run, our uncritical acceptance of the power of perseverance makes us more callous to the injustices of the world. We can't fix everything—but the things we *can* fix, we must.

———————

So, to quit or not to quit?

"There's no formula for knowing when you should persist and when you should change course," Wendy Kaminer tells me. "Sometimes you need to keep pushing forward. Sometimes you need to stop."

It's not an easy judgment to make, however, because the deck is stacked against quitting. The choice to *not* quit—to keep going even when it doesn't feel right—has an unfair advantage over the choice to give up and try something else. Perseverance comes to us all tricked out in an appealing package. It's routinely presented as a moral force in the march of civilization, as the thing that puts rockets in the sky and ships in the ocean and vaccines in syringes, while quitting is equated with inertia and slovenly failure.

Yet once grit is stripped of its ribbons, of that veneer of virtue, we can decide with greater clarity—as other animals do and always have done, on the basis of what ensures their survival—our best next move.

Hence, I hope you'll ask yourself this the next time you're conflicted over whether to keep going or to quit, to pivot or to stick with it: Am I making my choice based on what I believe will work for me or on the fear of being officially designated a quitter if I give up? Am I choosing what I truly want or what somebody else thinks is best for me?

And maybe you'll consider another question, too: If you *were* to be dubbed a quitter, what's the harm? If we begin to see quitting in a different light and stop automatically equating it with failure, its potential may emerge—its promise as a life strategy. It might even sound like a compliment.

"When you quit, you're choosing life itself," says Spiotta, author of *Wayward*. "To be alive is to take these leaps. If you can't imagine another life, you're quitting on your obligation to be alive."

———————

By the time he died in 2020, actor Clark Middleton had proven that you can jettison an attitude—in the case of someone with a physical limitation, as he often stated in interviews, it's the temptation of self-pity—just as surely as you can quit a job or anything else, and that the act of quitting can free you. Juvenile idiopathic arthritis left Middleton with severe mobility issues and an unusually short stature, but none of that got in the way of his long career as a highly accomplished actor in films such as *Kill Bill: Vol. 2* and TV series such as *Twin Peaks* and *The Blacklist*.

Talking about his disability to an advocacy group, Middleton once said, "By thinking of it as something that you're fighting you almost become a victim to it, and it has power over you... So I suggest reframing it, and thinking about befriending it, and learning to dance with it."

That's an exhilarating idea, and one with relevance to quitting: You can take something that others may see as a negative, as a dreadful fate, and you can agree with them and treat it as an adversary, a thing to be denied, repudiated, beaten back, subdued. Or you can make peace with it and carve out space for it and treat it as just another part of your life.

You can embrace quitting. You can dance with it.

PERMISSION SLIP

You've been thinking of that urge to quit as the enemy, as something you must vanquish. But try to envision quitting as your friend and ally, as part of a long-term, creative, dynamic strategy for your life, a life filled with radiant possibilities. You can quit as often as you need to, as often as you feel you must. Listen to your conscience as well as your heart. And thrive.

Afterword

A great truth is a truth whose opposite is
also a great truth.

—*Niels Bohr*

Quitting—more specifically, not being able to do so—defined my father's life.

James Keller was a smoker from the age of fifteen. He grew up poor in West Virginia. Smoking, I imagine, was one of the few ways an Appalachian boy could achieve the kind of cool swagger so beloved by adolescents, no matter where they come from. By the time he was an adult with a wife and three kids, my father had concluded that smoking constituted the great tragedy of his life. But it was too late. He couldn't quit.

I don't have to guess about his hatred of the habit; he didn't conceal it. When he caught my older sister, Cathy, then sixteen, hiding in the garage to try a few exploratory puffs on a Marlboro, he said to her, more in sorrow than in anger, "I'd rather see you with your hand cut off than see you holding that cigarette." He didn't really mean it, of course; he just wanted to shock her. A mathematician with a logical, rigorous mind, he wasn't typically given to such hyperbole, but he was heartbroken over what smoking had done to him. He didn't want to see her go down the same road.

A large part of my childhood thus was spent living in the shadow of quitting. I don't know you, but I'm guessing that maybe you, too, lived in a similar shadow. So many of us do. And maybe you, too, had a parent or other family member who tried to quit an unhealthy habit. Maybe it was smoking in the case of your family, too, or maybe it was alcohol or illegal drugs or rage.

I watched my father try, with a frustration that grew over the decades, to renounce cigarettes. A pattern emerged: First there would be the ritual throwing away of all the packs stored in what was uncreatively called "the cigarette drawer" in the kitchen. And then, a few days or sometimes even hours later, my father, with a wince of resignation, would light up the cigarette he'd stashed away, just in case.

Everything went back to normal. The cigarette drawer was quietly restocked.

He was never secretive about his relapses. They always occurred out in the open. He was clearly ashamed of himself, humbled by what he saw as abject weakness, as a character flaw—but he owned up to it, every time. And there were many, many times. So many that I lost count. Quit and resume, quit and resume. Rinse and repeat.

My father wasn't wrong about smoking and ruin. He died of lung cancer at age fifty-one at Ohio State University Hospital, some nine months after he'd been diagnosed. I watched him take his final breath. By then—after the chemo and the radiation—he looked eighty-one, not fifty-one.

But there's more to my father's life than his inability to quit smoking. More than his doomed attempts to set aside the cigarettes forever. More than his failures.

God knows, I wish he'd been able to stop smoking, for my sake as well as his—I've missed him so in the years since his death. But I also wish that he hadn't judged his life by this terrible thing he couldn't give up, this deadly habit that had him in its grip and wouldn't let go. He was so much more than his dependence on nicotine. To see James Keller that way is to give his addiction the final say, to let it write his epitaph. To offer pride of place to something he despised.

Better, I think, to recall the life he lived between his endless tries to quit: shooting baskets with me at the hoop in our driveway; building a deck on the back of the house because, like Willy Loman in *Death of a Salesman*, "he was a happy man with a batch of cement"; helping me and my sisters and my cousins with our math homework. That's what I want to remember.

Other family members still struggle with addiction issues, and I want the same for them and for anyone in any family who grapples with those demons. I want people to be known for their good hearts, not their bad habits. For their gifts, not their grievous shortcomings. Do I wish that anyone so bedeviled could rise above their ravenous appetites for substances that harm them? Of course I do. But it's not up to me. No matter how much we love or are loved, the most important battles are the ones we must fight alone.

In the end, no one's life—not my father's, not mine, not yours, nor the lives of the people we love—ought to be summarized by what we don't master, by the adversity we fail to overcome, by the challenges we aren't able, at long last, to meet. We all deserve better. Because most of us do the best we can. We stumble, we fall short, but we try. I know my father did.

I've spent this book arguing that quitting is good. How, then, can I also claim that quitting is *bad*—that I wish my father hadn't made quitting the focus of his life? That I wish he had quit on quitting? That I wish all of us could quit on quitting, too? Isn't that a contradiction?

Yes. And that's not a problem. As neuroscientist David J. Linden points out in a luminous essay about his terminal cancer diagnosis, our minds are fully capable of balancing mutually exclusive concepts:

> It is possible, even easy, to occupy two seemingly contradictory mental states at the same time...This runs counter to an old idea in neuroscience that we occupy one mental state at a time—we are either curious or fearful—we either "fight or flee"...based on some overall modulation of the nervous system.
>
> But our human brains are more nuanced than that, and so we can easily inhabit multiple, complex, even contradictory, cognitive and emotional states.

We can believe that quitting is a positive force in the world, that giving up cigarettes or binge drinking or unhealthy food (it's marble pound cake, not Marlboros, that constitutes my quitting challenge) is exemplary—and we can believe simultaneously that quitting is a negative force, and that we shouldn't be preoccupied by it, shouldn't beat ourselves up for the things we can't overcome no matter how hard we try.

That's why I hope that someday we'll be able to remove the stigma from quitting, in both directions. We're not horrible people if we're unable to quit a behavior that we should. And we're not heroes if we *are* able to quit—a job that's not working out, say, or a relationship that has turned sour. It may be a good thing to quit something if you want to do so, if you believe it will make you happier or healthier or both. But that's all it is: a good thing. One among many. And we're likely to need repeat attempts throughout our lives.

I wish my father hadn't berated himself for not being able to give up cigarettes. I wish that the issue of quitting hadn't haunted him as much as it did, because he was a man of many parts—granted, not all of them positive. He had a quick temper, but he was working on it. When he was riled, he could be cutting and sarcastic; that, too, was something he wanted to fix about himself. He loved, among many passions, the Green Bay Packers, country music, cashews straight out of the Planters jar and washed down with a Diet Coke, and the intricate and beguiling beauty of calculus.

Those were the things that truly defined him. Not quitting. And not the fact that he gave up on quitting, time and time again, and saw himself as a failure on account of it. He didn't quit smoking, and he didn't quit his job on the mathematics faculty of his university, despite the fact that his great gifts as a teacher were mostly overlooked there and he was woefully underpaid. He wanted to leave, but he never felt that the time was right.

And then there was no more time.

I wish he'd been able to quit both: the cigarettes and the job. Quitting the first would've brought him a longer life. Quitting the second would've enabled him to teach at another university, bringing him the respect his work deserved.

Sometimes we're able to throw off the yoke of an addiction, or of any behavior from which we'd love to free ourselves. Sometimes we're not. That doesn't make us evil or selfish or stupid. It makes us human. And an essential part of our humanity is an ability to recognize how much is simply out of anyone's control, how much is determined by genetic inheritance and by happenstance, and how much is forever unattainable, even with the aid of positive affirmations or a Fitbit.

The one thing we *can* control is forgiveness: forgiving ourselves and others for not always getting it right. And for failing. Because we *will* fail. We'll fail and we'll quit things again and again. We'll quit big things—as Bessel van der Kolk reports, more than three-quarters of the people who enter drug and alcohol rehab programs wash out—and we'll quit small things. Try as we might, we won't be the friends or partners or parents or neighbors or citizens we hope to be. We'll give up.

But that's not the end of the story. That's the *beginning* of the story. The real story. The one that's about empathy and understanding.

And maybe one day we'll come to the end of our furious and often futile striving, the end of our efforts to try and remake ourselves according to some abstract idea of what's desirable, what's cool. We'll give up on all of that. We'll be grateful for the gift of our contradictions, for the times when life requires us to be flexible, to let go of what's likely never coming true and to embrace the crooked beauty of compromise.

This book is dedicated to my niece, Annie Kate Goodwin, who had to learn how to do just that. Born and raised in the Midwest, her dream was to live in California. After graduating from law school, she was offered a job in San Francisco. She and her husband headed west. Three months later she was diagnosed with leukemia. She returned to Ohio for treatment. She died on September 12, 2019. She was thirty-three.

In the wake of her illness, Annie Kate had to radically adjust her expectations. She had to give up on the plans she'd made for her life and make other plans on the fly. But a changed dream is not necessarily a lesser one. And a short life needn't be a life without joy and meaning. A life of any length can be complete and beautiful. I love the words of Elliot Dallen, a British man who wrote essays for the *Guardian* in the months prior to his 2020 death of adrenocortical carcinoma at thirty-one: "A life, if lived well, is long enough."

Toward the end, everything Annie Kate wanted to do had to be compressed into a brutally brief interval—from telling the people she loved how much they meant to her to reveling in the work of the artists who had always captivated her, from Dostoevsky to Lady Gaga. And then it was over, her extraordinary life, a life that mustn't be measured in terms of tasks left undone, of roads left untraveled, but by the same simple metric that should be applied to all of our lives, whether we live to be 33 or 103: by the intensity of the passion with which we plunge into each new day and every new experience, quitting the old, embracing the thrillingly unfamiliar, over and over again.

Acknowledgments

To the friends who helped in the early stages of this book, brainstorming with me when it was barely a gleam in my mind's eye, I owe a warm debt of gratitude. Here goes: Joseph Hallinan, Patrick Reardon, Susan Phillips, Frank Donoghue, Suzanne Hyers, Mike Conklin, Marja Mills, Don Pierson, Lisa Keller, Robert Schmuhl, Clairan Ferrono, Elizabeth Berg, Cathy Dougherty, Carolyn Focht, and Lisa Knox.

I'm beholden as well to the dozens of people who generously shared with me the story of their lives, and to the scientists and scholars who endured my endless questions with good grace. To my regret, the pandemic meant that most of these interviews had to be conducted via email, phone, or Zoom, rather than face-to-face; I appreciate the lengths to which these very busy people went in order to accommodate my research requests. Any errors are my fault, not theirs.

My editor, Hannah Robinson, understood this book from the beginning. She brought to it her wit, her energy, her sensitivity, her peerless knowledge of pop culture, and her patience with a headstrong writer.

Notes

"You see, you cannot draw lines": Rohinton Mistry, *A Fine Balance* (New York: Vintage, 1997), pp. 228–29.

"No matter how far you have gone": Proverb quoted in *Speak, Okinawa: A Memoir* by Elizabeth Miki Brina, p. 1.

Introduction

"By doing nothing, we change nothing": John le Carré, *The Russia House* (New York: Knopf, 1989), p. 121.

"When scientists retest someone else's ideas": Tim Birkhead, *Bird Sense: What It's Like to Be a Bird* (New York: Walker & Co., 2012), p. xvii.

"Treating grit as a virtue": Dr. Adam Grant, email conversation with the author, October 9, 2021.

"From the 'lying flat' movement in China": Charlie Tyson, "The New Neurasthenia: How Burnout Became the Buzzword of the Moment," *The Baffler*, March 15, 2022, https://thebaffler.com/latest/the-new-neurasthenia-tyson.

"A new term": Rana Mitter, "Baby Bust: China's Looming Demographic Disaster," *Spectator*, August 6, 2022, https://spectator.co.uk/article/baby following-bust -chinas-looming-demographic-disaster.

In a buzzed-about 2021 essay: Cassady Rosenblum, "Work Is a False Idol," *New York Times*, August 22, 2021, https://www.nytimes.com/2021/08/22/opinion /lying-flat-work-rest.html.

"Suddenly talk of grit": Daniel T. Willingham, "Ask the Cognitive Scientist: 'Grit' Is Trendy, but Can It Be Taught?," *American Educator*, Summer 2016, p. 28.

In the first eight months of 2021: Patricia Kelly Yeo, " 'An Unbelievable Sense of Freedom': Why Americans Are Quitting in Record Numbers," *Guardian*, November 3, 2021, https://www.theguardian.com/us-news/2021/nov/03/an-unbeliev able-sense-of-freedom-why-americans-are-quitting-in-record-numbers.

"Not a soul outside her inner circle": Emma Kemp, "Ash Barty Announces Shock Retirement from Tennis at 25," *Guardian*, March 22, 2022, https://www.the guardian.com/sport/2022/mar/23/ash-barty-announces-shock-retirement -from-tennis-at-25.

"Quitting was an act of imagination": Jane Leavy, *Sandy Koufax: A Lefty's Legacy* (New York: HarperCollins, 2002), p. xvii.

"Americans often demonize quitting": Lindsay Crouse, "Don't Be Afraid to Quit. It Could Help You Win," *New York Times*, August 11, 2021, https:// www.nytimes.com/2021/08/11/opinion/molly-seidel-simone-biles-olympics .html.

"Hard work is likely the most": Tyson, "The New Neurasthenia."

"Honestly, I think the idea of quitting": Amy Dickinson, email conversation with the author, November 5, 2021.

More than a quarter of all students who started classes: Matt Krupnick, "More College Students Are Dropping Out during Covid. It Could Get Worse," *Guardian*, February 10, 2022, https://www.theguardian.com/us-news/2022 /feb/10/college-students-dropout-covid-pandemic.

Part I

"There's a point at which perseverance": Benjamin Wood, *The Ecliptic* (London: Scribner, 2015), p. 182.

Chapter One

"Misguided grit is the worst": John A. List, phone conversation with the author, March 11, 2022.

"Perseverance, in a biological sense": Jerry Coyne, phone conversation with the author, August 22, 2021.

"When times are hard, their lives depend": Jonathan Weiner, *The Beak of the Finch* (New York: Vintage, 1995), p. 63.

"That's a long time for a bird": Weiner, p. 60.

"exploratory networks made of tentacle-like": Merlin Sheldrake, *Entangled Life: How Fungi Make Our Worlds, Change Our Minds & Shape Our Futures* (New York: Random House, 2020), p. 15.

"Plants and animals seem intricately": Jerry Coyne, *Why Evolution Is True* (New York: Penguin Books, 2009), p. 1.

Among the experiments designed to test: Jennifer Ackerman, *The Genius of Birds* (New York: Penguin, 2016), pp. 20–37.

"The prevailing scientific view": Sheldrake, *Entangled Life*, p. 41.

"Here's how I imagined my resignation": Katie Heaney, "The Clock-Out Cure: For Those Who Can Afford It, Quitting Has Become the Ultimate Form of Self-Care," *New York*, May 11, 2021, https://www.thecut.com/2021/05/quit ting-your-job-as-self-care.html#_ga=2.207319898.893941653.1660245953-52 5243665.1660245953.

"Without the visual reinforcement of meat": Ackerman, *The Genius of Birds*, pp. 85–86.

"don't offer any direct benefits": Ackerman, p. 177.

"The cleverer males quickly discovered a novel strategy": Ackerman, p. 182.

"The more one learns about plants and animals": Coyne, *Why Evolution Is True*, p. 3.

"I was not physically capable": Simone Biles quoted by Camonghne Felix, "Simone Biles Chose Herself," *New York*, September 27, 2021, https://www.thecut .com/article/simone-biles-olympics-2021.html.

"To eat and not be eaten": Justin O. Schmidt, phone conversation with the author, August 23, 2021.

His experiments, the results of which he published in 2020: J. O. Schmidt, "Decision Making in Honeybees: A Time to Live, a Time to Die?," *Insectes Sociaux*, April 6, 2020. Published by International Union for the Study of Social Insects by Birkhäuser Verlag.

"Bees must make life-or-death decisions based on risk-benefit": Schmidt, conversation with the author.

According to news accounts, Brace said: Erin Cox, "University of the Cumberlands Sued for Wrestler's Death," *Times-Tribune*, August 26, 2021, https:// thetimestribune.com/news/local_news/university-of-the-cumberlands-sued -for-wrestlers-death/article_6945c063-1bcb-5061-b5ba-85376189577a.html.

"I didn't want to give up. It was so strange": Lynne Cox, *Swimming to Antarctica: Tales of a Long-Distance Swimmer* (New York: Harcourt, 2004), p. 119.

Our bodies, after all, are *designed* to tell us when to quit: Robert Sapolsky, *Why Zebras Don't Get Ulcers* (New York: W. H. Freeman, 1998), pp. 4–16.

"The most important job of the brain is to ensure our survival": Bessel van der Kolk, *The Body Keeps the Score: Brain, Mind, and Body in the Healing of Trauma* (New York: Penguin, 2014), p. 55.

"When I decided to get a divorce": Jody Alyn, phone conversation with the author, November 11, 2021.

"I had to leave. I couldn't keep doing the same things": Christine Sneed, phone conversation with the author, August 11, 2021.

"comes to us the same way it comes to the bird": Emily Nagoski and Amelia Nagoski, *Burnout: The Secret to Unlocking the Stress Cycle* (New York: Ballantine, 2019), p. 47.

"We live in a culture that values 'self-control,' 'grit,' and persistence": Nagoski and Nagoski, p. 47.

Chapter Two

"I think intention and willpower": June Huh, quoted by Jordana Cepelewicz in "He Dropped Out to Become a Poet. Now He's Won a Fields Medal," *Quanta Magazine*, July 5, 2022, https://www.quantamagazine.org/June-huh-high-school-dropout-wins-the-fields-medal-20220705/.

"You can pose the narrative as heroic change": Todd Parker, phone conversation with the author, August 24, 2021.

"For humans, there are many ways in which we abandon behaviors": Misha Ahrens, phone conversation with the author, October 25, 2021. All quotations are from this interview unless otherwise noted.

"Even the basic operational principles": Florian Engert quoted by Ariel Sabar in "How a Transparent Fish May Help Decode the Brain," *Smithsonian Magazine*, July 2015, https://www.smithsonianmag.com/science-nature/How-transparent-fish-may-help-decode-brain-180955734/.

This enabled them to "look at what *fueled* neural activity": van der Kolk, *The Body Keeps the Score*, pp. 39–40.

"Neurons—influenced by genes, the environment": Michael Bruchas, phone conversation with the author, September 2, 2021. All quotations are from this interview unless otherwise noted.

"The cells exchange messages in the form of electrical pulses": Sabar, "How a Transparent Fish May Help Decode the Brain."

"To read the minds of baby zebrafish": Sabar.

Scientists now believe, however, that glial cells: Elena Renken, "Glial Brain Cells, Long in Neurons' Shadow, Reveal Hidden Powers," *Quanta Magazine*, January 27, 2020, https://www.quantamagazine.org/glial-brain-cells-long-in-neurons-shadow-reveal-hidden-powers-20200127/.

According to a report on the experiment published in 2019: Yu Mu et al., "Glia Accumulate Evidence That Actions Are Futile and Suppress Unsuccessful Behavior," *Cell* 178, no. 1 (June 27, 2019).

"I decided that I would understand Einstein's theory": Jeremy Bernstein, "Childe Bernstein to Relativity Came," in *My Einstein*, ed. John Brockman (New York: Pantheon, 2006), pp. 156–57.

In 2019, Bruchas and his team reported a breakthrough: "Researchers Discover the Science behind Giving Up," UW Medicine Newsroom, July 25, 2019, https://newsroom.uw.edu/news/researchers-discover-science-behind-giving.

"In order for the brain to know if it should change": Thilo Womelsdorf, phone conversation with the author, September 2, 2012. All quotations are from this interview unless otherwise noted.

"These neurons seem to help the brain circuits": Kianoush Banaie Boroujeni, quoted in "Neuroscientists at Vanderbilt Identify the Brain Cells That Help Humans Adapt to Change," Vanderbilt University Research News, July 15, 2020, https://news.vanderbilt.edu/2020/07/15/neuroscientists-at-vanderbilt-identify-the-brain-cells-that-help-humans-adapt-to-change/.

"Some of the time we are indeed": Robert M. Sapolsky, *Behave: The Biology of Humans at Our Best and Worst* (New York: Penguin, 2017), p. 11.

"The social environment interacts": van der Kolk, *The Body Keeps the Score*, p. 35.

"Culture is like the chalk and limestone": Bernd Heinrich, *Life Everlasting: The Animal Way of Death* (New York: Houghton Mifflin Harcourt, 2012), p. 171.

Chapter Three

"It will be a little messy": Nora Ephron, 1996 commencement address at Wellesley College, commencement archives, https://www.wellesley.edu/events/commencement/archives/1996commencement.

"Art invites identification": Matthew Specktor, *Always Crashing in the Same Car: On Art, Crisis, & Los Angeles, California* (Portland, OR: Tin House, 2021), p. 207.

"I believe art and life": Specktor, pp. 213–14.

"There's a reason": Emily Zemler, email conversation with the author, February 16, 2022.

"I think most people underestimate": Dr. Devon Price, email conversation with the author, May 25, 2022.

"The character I played [in *The Colbys*] was Constance": Barbara Stanwyck, in a letter dated October 24, 1986, to film students at the University of Wyoming. Reprinted by permission of the university's American Heritage Center.

"And saying yes to this version": Dana Spiotta, *Wayward* (New York: Knopf, 2021), p. 13.

"Quitting is a negative word": Dana Spiotta, phone conversation with the author, January 7, 2022.

"Our history of giving up—that is to say": Adam Phillips, "On Giving Up," *London Review of Books* 44, no. 1 (January 6, 2022), https://www.lrb.co.uk /the-paper/v44/n01/adam-phillips/on-giving-up.

"What is it, this nameless, inscrutable": Herman Melville, *Moby-Dick or, The Whale* (Indianapolis: Bobbs Merrill, 1964), p. 685.

In Verdi's *La Traviata*, Violetta gives up: Roger Pines, email conversation with the author, January 16, 2022.

"When I was eighteen, I just thought, 'I'm not going to play'": Diane Casey, phone conversation with the author, April 22, 2022.

"At last, in reply to my urgings": Herman Melville, *Four Short Novels* (New York: Bantam Books, 1959), p. 25.

"I pull the bow": John Updike, "A&P," *The Early Stories: 1953–1975* (New York: Random House, 2004), p. 601.

"We are not just the product of our genes": Heinrich, *Life Everlasting*, p. 194.

"Much like the Horatio Alger novels of the past": Devon Price, *Laziness Does Not Exist: A Defense of the Exhausted, Exploited, and Overworked* (New York: Atria, 2021), p. 27.

"When massively successful stars attribute their good fortune": Price, pp. 29–30.

Part II

"Holding up hard work": Adam Grant, email conversation with the author, October 9, 2021.

Chapter Four

"You know the saying": Stephen J. Dubner, *Freakonomics Radio* podcast, "The Upside of Quitting," September 30, 2011.

"It was definitely a very dark time": Heather Stone, phone conversation with the author, November 21, 2021.

"He invented the self-help market at just the right time": Dr. Peter Sinnema, phone conversation with the author, September 24, 2021.

"patron saint of the self-help movement": Walter Isaacson, *Benjamin Franklin: An American Life* (New York: Simon & Schuster, 2003), p. 484.

"the reigning queen of the world of life coaching": Rachel Monroe, "I'm a Life Coach, You're a Life Coach: The Rise of an Unregulated Industry," *Guardian*, October 6, 2021, https://www.theguardian.com/lifeandstyle/2021/oct/06/life-coaching-brooke-castillo-unregulated-industry.

"Our culture is imbued with the belief": Julia Samuel, *Grief Works: Stories of Life, Death, and Surviving* (New York: Simon & Schuster, 2017), p. xxiv.

"We are a forward-looking, future-preoccupied": Sharon O'Brien, introduction to *My Ántonia*, by Willa Cather (New York: Penguin, 1994), pp. viii–ix.

"heroic individualism": Brad Stulberg, *The Practice of Groundedness: A Transformative Path to Success That Feeds—Not Crushes—Your Soul* (New York: Portfolio, 2021), p. 10.

"On the morning of April 6, 2007, I was lying on the floor": Arianna Huffington, *Thrive: The Third Metric to Redefining Success and Creating a New Life of Well-Being, Wisdom, and Wonder* (New York: Harmony Books, 2015), p. 1.

"It's just wrapped in different paper today" and **"There are all kinds of external dashboards in life"**: Stulberg, email conversation with the author, November 10, 2021.

"There are all kinds of external dashboards in life": Brad Stulberg, email conversation with the author, November 10, 2021.

"Unless one is lying to oneself, life is a hotbed": Matthew Specktor, "Enter the Dream Factory: Christine Sneed in Conversation with Matthew Specktor," interview by Christine Sneed, *The Millions*, June 8, 2021, https://themillions.com/2021/07/enter-the-dream-factory-christine-sneed-in-conversation-with-matthew-specktor.html.

"Men must necessarily be the active agents": Samuel Smiles, *Self-Help: With Illustrations of Character and Conduct* (New York: Oxford University Press, 2008), p. 22.

"The road of human welfare": Smiles, p. 90.

"Critics of self-help": Anna Katharina Schaffner, "Top 10 Books about Self-Improvement," *Guardian*, December 29, 2021, https://www.theguardian.com/books/2021/dec/29/top-10-books-about-self-improvement-anna-katharina-schaffner-the-art-of-self-improvement-new-year-resolutions.

"People walk around bewildered": Wendy Kaminer, phone conversation with the author, November 30, 2021.

"Practical dreamers do not quit!": Napoleon Hill, *Think and Grow Rich* (New York: Fawcett Crest, 1960), p. 38.

"Thoughts which are mixed with any of the feelings": Hill, p. 53.

"No man is ever whipped, until he quits—in his own mind": Hill, p. 103.

"The majority of people are ready to throw their aims": Hill, p. 151.

"If one does not possess persistence": Hill, p. 155.

"indifference, usually reflected in one's readiness": Hill, p. 158.

"Believe in yourself!": Norman Vincent Peale, *The Power of Positive Thinking* (New York: Fawcett Crest, 1952), p. 13.

"It was crap": Paul Peterson, phone conversation with the author, November 30, 2021.

"My whole life has been a soul search": Ron Rhoden, conversation with the author, November 3, 2021.

"There's no need for a mad rush": Tracy Wilk, quoted in "LinkedIn Asked People to Give Advice to Their 20-Year-Old Selves" by Jessica Stillman, *Inc.*, July 22, 2021, https://www.inc.com/jessica-stillman/linkedin-career-advice-jeff-bezos .html.

"Every time I quit something": Rick McVey, phone conversation with the author, September 8, 2021.

Chapter Five

"Fundamental randomness is unbearable": Anton Zeilinger, "Einstein and Absolute Reality," in *My Einstein*, ed. John Brockman (New York: Pantheon, 2006), p. 127.

"I'd never walked into an animal shelter": Sharon Harvey, phone conversation with the author, September 14, 2021.

"that dark miracle of chance": Thomas Wolfe, *Look Homeward, Angel* (New York: Scribner, 1929), p. 5.

"a puzzling limitation of our mind": Daniel Kahneman, *Thinking, Fast and Slow* (New York: Farrar, Straus and Giroux, 2011), p. 14.

"It helps to have long-term goals, but what you really need": Dan Cnossen, quoted by Dave Sheinin in "A Wounded Warrior's Grueling Path to Paralympic Gold," *Washington Post*, March 4, 2022, https://www.washingtonpost.com /sports/olympics/2022/03/11/dan-cnossen-navy-seal-paralympics-biathlon/.

"The lesson I learned is that you don't always have control": Michele Weldon, phone conversation with the author, September 7, 2021.

"The short version is that my father left our family": Amy Dickinson, email conversation with the author, November 5, 2021.

"I was in denial": Christine Broquet, phone conversation with the author, July 28, 2021.

"And I filed as many stories and news spots": Howard Berkes, email conversation with the author, January 16, 2022.

"There are no geniuses": Emily Langer, "Justus Rosenberg, Holocaust rescuer, dies at 100," *Washington Post*, November 19, 2021, https://www.washington post.com/obituaries/2021/11/19/justus-rosenberg-dead/.

"If he had been a few yards away from where he was": George F. Will, "The Goodness of Bob Dole," *Washington Post*, December 5, 2021, https://www .washingtonpost.com/opinions/2021/12/05/goodness-of-bob-dole-george -will/.

Chapter Six

"The flip side of positivity": Barbara Ehrenreich, *Bright-Sided: How the Relentless Promotion of Positive Thinking Has Undermined America* (New York: Metropolitan Books, 2009), p. 8.

"The story of the Bronx blaze": Ross Barkan, "Why Is New York City's Mayor Blaming Tenants for the Deadliest Fire in a Century?" *Guardian*, January 13, 2022, https://www.theguardian.com/commentisfree/2022/jan/13/why-is-new-york-citys-mayor-blaming-tenants-for-the-deadliest-fire-in-decades.

"Self-improvement books do not work": Dr. Micki McGee, phone conversation with the author, December 19, 2021.

"The ideal of individual success": Micki McGee, *Self-Help, Inc.: Makeover Culture in American Life* (New York: Oxford University Press, 2005), p. 13.

"The past year [was] the best time in history": Eli Saslow, "The Moral Calculations of a Billionaire," *Washington Post*, January 30, 2022, https://www.wash ingtonpost.com/nation/2022/01/30/moral-calculations-billionaire/.

"It's in the same category as": Phillip Martin, email conversation with the author, May 26, 2022.

"It was embarrassing. Not having a set plan": Joe Rodriguez, email conversation with the author, September 3, 2021.

"So much of self-help holds *us* responsible": Wendy Simonds, phone conversation with the author, September 17, 2021.

"Drug addiction and alcoholism": Jennifer Haigh, *Mercy Street* (New York: Ecco, 2022), p. 7.

"Cultures get transformed not deliberately or programmatically": Louis Menand, *The Free World: Art and Thought in the Cold War* (New York: Farrar, Straus and Giroux, 2021), p. xiii.

"When wealth is passed off": Sarah Kendzior, *The View from Flyover Country: Dispatches from the Forgotten America* (New York: Macmillan, 2018), p. xi.

Chapter Seven

A journalist asked, "Was this the equivalent of": Kyle Porter, "2022 Masters: A Legend Who Only Defined Success as Victory, Tiger Woods Inspires by Refus-ing to Stop Competing," CBS Sports, April 10, 2022, https://www.cbssports .com/golf/news/2022-masters-a-legend-who-only-defined-success-as-victory -tiger-woods-inspires-by-refusing-to-stop-competing/.

"doing the least amount of work": Stephen Daisley, "Why Everyone Should Be 'Quiet Quitting,'" *Spectator*, August 13, 2022, https://www.spectator.co.uk /article/why-everyone-should-be-quiet-quitting-.

"I have never made a decision such as": Paula Cocozza, "A New Start after 60: 'I Became a Psychotherapist at 69 and Found My Calling,'" *Guardian*, March 7, 2022, https://www.theguardian.com/lifeandstyle/2022/mar/07/a-new-start -after-60-i-became-a-psychotherapist-at-69-and-found-my-calling.

"You have to fight this binary thinking": Leidy Klotz, phone conversation with the author, December 8, 2021.

"I was in my boss's office and getting chewed out": Lori Rader-Day, phone con-versation with the author, June 30, 2021.

"It's tough being me": Dave Allen, phone conversation with the author, October 20, 2021.

"But what if they harbored a secret desire to stop": David W. Chen, "A Cham-pion Swimmer Found a New Life on the Rocks," *New York Times*, August 18, 2021, https://www.nytimes.com/2021/08/18/sports/swimming-champion-rock -climbing-freedom.html.

"When I was a boy, my parents would turn their backs": Franklin Foer, *How Soccer Explains the World: An Unlikely Theory of Globalization* (New York: Harper, 2004), p. 1.

"Told in retrospect by popular media": David Epstein, *Range: Why Generalists Triumph in a Specialized World* (New York: Riverhead, 2019), p. 287.

"At the last minute I changed my mind": Epstein, p. 142.

"found that people who switch jobs more frequently": Derek Thompson, "Hot Streaks in Your Career Don't Happen by Accident," *Atlantic*, November 1, 2021, https://www.theatlantic.com/ideas/archive/2021/11/hot-streaks-in-your-career-dont-happen-by-accident/620514/.

"it turned out that virtually every person": Epstein, pp. 153-154.

"reevaluation and rerouting": Arianne Cohen, "Why You Should Quit Your Job after 10 Years," *Bloomberg Businessweek*, June 24, 2022, https://www .bloomberg.com/news/articles/2022-06-24/make-a-career-change-every-10 -or-so-years-experts-say.

"Franklin is the absolute exemplar of cognitive nimbleness": Edward Gray, phone conversation with the author, October 21, 2021.

"Steve encouraged him to think": Katharine Q. Seelye, "Greg Steltenpohl, Pioneer in Plant-Based Drinks, Dies at 66," *New York Times*, March 19, 2021, https://www.nytimes.com/2021/03/19/business/greg-steltenpohl-dead.html.

"jeers, hisses, catcalls": Leon Edel, *Henry James* (New York: Harper & Row, 1985), p. 420.

"It is miserable in me to care at all about priority": Janet Browne, *Charles Darwin: The Power of Place* (Princeton, NJ: Princeton University Press, 2002), p. 38.

"I am quite prostrated & can do nothing": Browne, p. 37.

"For so long, Darwin had been hemmed in": Browne, p. 48.

"a lasting work of art": Browne, p. 55.

Chapter Eight

"Strategic quitting is the secret of successful organizations": Seth Godin, *CBS Sunday Morning*, May 5, 2019.

"This definitely wasn't like the thing": Rachel Maddow, "Rachel Maddow on Her Critics: 'Your Hatred Makes Me Stronger. Come on! Give Me More!,'" interview by David Smith, *Guardian*, February 2, 2020, https://www.theguardian.com/media/2020/feb/02/rachel-maddow-on-her-critics-your-hatred-makes-me-stronger-come-on-give-me-more.

"I mean, I remember in the 2008 recession": Betsey Stevenson, transcript, *The Ezra Klein Show* podcast, "Welcome to the 'Take This Job and Shove It' Economy," June 18, 2021, p. 3.

"I started to get ignored": Lucinda Hahn, phone conversation with the author, December 22, 2021.

the last big adventure: Described at length in Edmund Morris, *Edison* (New York: Random House, 2019), pp. 53–82.

"He seemed unable to drive past a weed patch": Morris, p. 53.

"My father-in-law": Cathy Ballenger, phone conversation with the author, April 8, 2022.

"isn't a straightforward progression": Guy Dove, phone conversation with the author, February 2, 2022.

"The way I look at it, we don't quit enough": John A. List, phone conversation with the author, March 11, 2022.

"By the end of that weekend": John A. List, *The Voltage Effect: How to Make Good Ideas Great and Great Ideas Scale* (New York: Currency, 2022), p. 185.

"getting good at quitting": List, *The Voltage Effect*, p. 187.

"He made those across the table": Eliot Brown and Maureen Farrell, *The Cult of We: WeWork, Adam Neumann, and the Great Startup Delusion* (New York: Crown, 2021), pp. 337–38.

"I've heard this countless times": Grant, email conversation with the author, October 9, 2021.

"It's a huge struggle": Ruth Sternberg, phone conversation with the author, August 13, 2021.

"Choosing the intense but brief pain": List, *The Voltage Effect*, p. 200.

"I have no regrets now about anything I've quit": Jack Zimmerman, phone conversation with the author, August 30, 2021.

"Quitting Joie de Vivre": Chip Conley, email conversation with the author, December 16, 2021.

"Sometimes it's better to go in blind": Mike and Lesli Mautz, conversation with the author, November 7, 2021.

to average a new invention every eleven days for forty years: Morris, *Edison*, p. 272.

"Am pretty well burned out": Morris, pp. 166–67.

Chapter Nine

"I hope you live a life": Often mistakenly attributed to F. Scott Fitzgerald, but it doesn't appear in his work and most people agree it was written by Eric Roth, screenwriter of the 2008 adaptation of Fitzgerald's short story "The Curious Case of Benjamin Button." The Falmouth Public Library in Falmouth, Massachusetts, ran an item about the misattribution in a 2011 blog post and continues to update it under the heading "The Curious Case of Misquotation." The entire multiyear thread is a fun read.

"Nobody in my family had ever earned": Stephany Rose Spaulding, phone conversation with the author, November 23, 2021.

"There's a difference between choosing to stop and *quitting*": Kristen Dieffenbach, phone conversation with the author, November 10, 2021.

"I was working on a story in the newsroom": Robin Yocum, conversation with the author, September 28, 2021.

"My husband and I and our five-year-old son": Bonnie Miller Rubin, phone conversation with the author, August 10, 2021.

"I was like, 'Hell, yes!'": Heidi Stevens, phone conversation with the author, November 20, 2021.

"She was supportive when I did gymnastics": June Stevens, phone conversation with the author, December 27, 2021.

"a neighbor drove there every day": Lewis Hanes, phone conversation with the author, November 28, 2021.

"Decision-making is tough": Eric J. Johnson, *The Elements of Choice: Why the Way We Decide Matters* (New York: Riverhead, 2021), p. 291.

"A lot of my decisions I think of as": Eric J. Johnson, phone conversation with the author, December 16, 2021.

"It took a while for me to make the leap": Susan Warren, phone conversation with the author, December 30, 2021.

"I never believed in just letting someone struggle": Marge Galloway, conversation with the author, September 25, 2021.

"There was a tense evening sitting around": Lara Weber, phone conversation with the author, August 19, 2021.

"They took baths when the creek": Gail Hetzler, phone conversation with the author, October 12, 2021.

Chapter Ten

"Visibility these days": Michaela Coel, quoted in Shirley Li's "The Quietest Emmys Speech Was the Loudest," *Atlantic*, September 20, 2021, https://www.theatlantic.com/culture/archive/2021/09/michaela-coel-emmys-2021/620130/.

"Girl, Wash Your Timeline": Katherine Rosman, "Girl, Wash Your Timeline," *New York Times*, April 29, 2021, https://www.nytimes.com/2021/04/29/style/rachel-hollis-tiktok-video.html.

"Today a single slip": Cathy O'Neil, *The Shame Machine: Who Profits in the New Age of Humiliation* (New York: Crown, 2022), pp. 96–97.

QuitTok: Sean Sanders and Jessica Mendoza, "'Quit-Tok': 'The Great Resignation' Hits Social Media," *Good Morning America*, December 9, 2021, https://www.goodmorningamerica.com/living/story/tiktok-publicly-resign-jobs-81645086.

"I have never started anything": Ashley Owusu, quoted in "Brenda Frese Downplays High-Profile Transfers, Restocks Maryland's Roster" by Kareem Copeland, *Washington Post*, May 13, 2022, https://www.washingtonpost.com/sports/2022/05/13/maryland-womens-basketball-transfers-brenda-frese/.

"Social media enables identities": Aaron Balick, email conversation with the author, February 28, 2022.

"I'm here today because I believe": Dan Milmo, "Frances Haugen Takes on Facebook: The Making of a Modern US Hero," *Guardian*, October 10, 2021, https://www.theguardian.com/technology/2021/oct/10/frances-haugen-takes -on-facebook-the-making-of-a-modern-us-hero.

"Some elect not to go public": Patrick Radden Keefe, "The Bounty Hunter," *New Yorker*, January 24, 2022, p. 34.

"The Facebook post was scary": Melissa Allison, phone conversation with the author, August 10, 2021.

"So much happened between his so-called": Robert Schmuhl, phone conversation with the author, January 12, 2022.

"Twitter is a red light, blinking": Caitlin Flanagan, "You Really Need to Quit Twitter," *Atlantic*, July 5, 2021, https://www.theatlantic.com/ideas/archive/2021 /07/twitter-addict-realizes-she-needs-rehab/619343/.

"There is a burgeoning backlash": Moya Lothian-McLean, "I Built a Life on Oversharing—Until I Saw Its Costs, and Learned the Quiet Thrill of Privacy," *Guardian*, May 2, 2022, https://www.theguardian.com/commentisfree/2022 /may/02/life-oversharing-costs-thrill-privacy-social-media-journalism.

"These days, divorce is seen as": Freya India, "Adele and the Strange Glamorisa- tion of Divorce," *Spectator*, May 10, 2022, https://www.spectator.co.uk/article /no-adele-divorce-isn-t-glamorous.

Chapter Eleven

"Giving up hope has given me back": Keith Kahn-Harris, "I Gave Up Hope of a Cure for My Chronic Condition," *Guardian*, July 28, 2022, https://theguardian.com/commentisfree/2022/jul/28/hope-cure-chronic -condition-identity-disability.

"Honestly, I don't think I had ever quit": Dickinson, email conversation with the author, November 5, 2021.

That record included the moment: Susan Stamberg, "Denied a Stage, She Sang for a Nation," NPR, April 9, 2014, https://www.npr.org/2014/04/09/298760473 /denied-a-stage-she-sang-for-a-nation.

"With quitting, you're putting yourself": Klotz, phone conversation with the author, December 8, 2021.

"Our culture teaches us to focus": van der Kolk, *The Body Keeps the Score*, p. 80.

"By the time I physically left": Connie Schultz, phone conversation with the author, August 23, 2021.

"It was killing my soul": Patty Bills, phone conversation with the author, October 28, 2021.

"Within the hour, my dorm phone rings": Tim Bannon, phone conversation with the author, August 24, 2021.

"Over my life I've seen friends fail to leave": Julian Barnes, *The Only Story* (New York: Knopf, 2018), pp. 87–88.

"Quit to what?": Dr. Gaurava Agarwal, phone conversation with the author, January 4, 2022.

"I'd reached a plateau at Stanford": Glen Worthey, phone conversation with the author, September 5, 2021.

"All night long the gears of delivery trucks": Margaret Renkl, *Late Migrations: A Natural History of Love and Loss* (Minneapolis: Milkweed, 2019), p. 113.

"I think most of my own happiness": Renkl, p. 119.

"Quitting gets a bad rap in life": Derek Thompson, "What Quitters Understand about the Job Market," *Atlantic*, June 21, 2021, https://www.theatlantic.com/ideas/archive/2021/06/quitting-your-job-economic-optimism/619242/.

"They don't realize how much time": Rich Muller, quoted in "Notes from a Parallel Universe," by Jennifer Kahn, *The Best American Science Writing 2003* (New York: HarperCollins, 2003), p. 118.

"Flexibility is not a passive process": George A. Bonanno, *The End of Trauma: How the New Science of Resilience Is Changing How We Think about PTSD* (New York: Basic Books, 2021), p. 16.

"Most people are resilient": Bonanno, p. 18.

"When a strategy is not working": Bonanno, p. 215.

"There's no formula for knowing": Kaminer, phone conversation with the author, November 30, 2021.

"When you quit, you're choosing": Spiotta, phone conversation with the author, January 7, 2022.

"By thinking of it as something that you're fighting": Clark Middleton. These comments came in a video Middleton made for the Arthritis Foundation, https://blog.arthritis.org/living-with-arthritis/life-legacy-clark-middleton/.

Afterword

"A great truth is a truth": Niels Bohr, quoted in *Coming of Age in the Milky Way* by Timothy Ferris (New York: William Morrow, 1988), p. 381.

"he was a happy man": Arthur Miller, *Death of a Salesman*, in *The Portable Arthur Miller* (New York: Viking, 1971), p. 132.

"It is possible, even easy, to occupy": David J. Linden, "A Neuroscientist Prepares for Death," *Atlantic*, December 30, 2021, https://www.theatlantic.com/ideas /archive/2021/12/terminal-cancer-neuroscientist-prepares-death/621114/.

"A life, if lived well": Elliot Dallen, "At 31, I Have Just Weeks to Live. Here's What I Want to Pass On," *Guardian*, September 7, 2020, https://www.theguardian .com/commentisfree/2020/sep/07/terminal-cancer-live-cancer-life-death.

books to help you live a good life

Join the conversation and tell
us how you live a #goodlife

🐦 @yellowkitebooks
📘 YellowKiteBooks
📌 Yellow Kite Books
📷 YellowKiteBooks